HANDWRITING IN PSYCHOLOGICAL INTERPRETATIONS

HANDWRITING IN PSYCHOLOGICAL INTERPRETATIONS

By

ARTHUR G. HOLT

Doctor of Jurisprudence

Second Printing

CHARLES C THOMAS • PUBLISHER
Springfield · Illinois · U.S.A.

Published and Distributed Throughout the World by
CHARLES C THOMAS · PUBLISHER
Bannerstone House
301-327 East Lawrence Avenue, Springfield, Illinois, U.S.A.

© *1965, by* CHARLES C THOMAS · PUBLISHER
ISBN 0-398-00864-7
Library of Congress Catalog Card Number: 64-24048

With THOMAS BOOKS careful attention is given to all details of manufacturing and design. It is the Publisher's desire to present books that are satisfactory as to their physical qualities and artistic possibilities and appropriate for their particular use. THOMAS BOOKS will be true to those laws of quality that assure a good name and good will.

First Printing, 1965
Second Printing, 1974

Printed in the United States of America
N-1

To Edith, my wife
and closest collaborator

PREFACE

For many of us, the looks of people, their habit of emphasizing attractive virtues, is an indication that they reflect a sterling character. Our expectations are often so unrealistic that we are inclined to attribute assets to others they do not possess. We often maintain that people are fine people, kind-hearted, decent and wonderful and are greatly disappointed when we learn the hard way that such a view is not justified.

Many of us judge our fellow men only by what they do for us, look at them from a mere selfish standpoint, and condemn those who refuse to cater to our wishes. At the root of these faulty observations is the fact that we do not even know ourselves, are seldom objective in judging our own failings, and are greatly misinformed about others.

We are afraid of revealing our shortcomings for we assume that if others became aware of them, our prestige would decline. Thus, we try to conceal them at any cost, even at the cost of depleting our nervous energy. Instead of courageously admitting our own weaknesses, we are inclined to delude ourselves.

Many of us condemn character traits in others for which we find excuses in ourselves. Many of us try to protect ourselves by not admitting weak points in persons to whom we have taken a liking. We prefer to see them as we would like to see them, without blemish.

To have met an unforgettable character is a personal evaluation which grows out of memorable experiences with a certain person. It does not necessarily mean that he is angelic. Others may have had most trying experiences with him. We are inclined to overlook the fact that many whom we consider bad can be lovely and devoted to certain people and, in contrast to this, the opposite side of their nature may tell against others. We are inclined to overlook a marked discrepancy in people between appearance and reality. Therefore, it is risky to judge a person according to his outer appearance only because many of us can hide our true nature for a long period of time. How else could it happen that in judging a certain person the estimate may be easily too high or too low. It may raise him to the level of a superman or bring him down to the level of an evil doer, depending on the nature of the person who makes the evaluation and what moral standard he requires from others. As a matter of fact different people make different demands in regard to their fellow men. There are some whose manner of acting to them does not seem unconventional or unprincipled, while others believe that they cannot reconcile certain actions with their own ethical standard.

Why be deceived about ourselves and our fellow men? Why not see ourselves and others realistically to avoid later disappointment and to arrest bitter and desponding thoughts? Why not better assume from the onset that to be human is to have more faults than virtues? Let us not fool ourselves that there are sterling characters on earth. There is only one Creator, and he lives in Heaven. No one of us is perfect, and there is no one who can be called completely good or bad.

Would it not be better to protect ourselves from our own weaknesses and to utilize our strength for our own benefit? To achieve this end in this world of ever changing values knowledge of man is as essential as is technical know-how.

Knowledge of man makes it easier for us to observe the different natures of people, to understand and sympathize with them, to make allowances for their weaknesses. When we notice their shortcomings and take them into stride, others will find it difficult to harm us. In doing so, we will then recognize that we also have weaknesses. This recognition will lead to greater self-control, to self-understanding, and to a better management of the complexities of life.

When we know ourselves well, when we learn to accept our own faults as natural, do not fear them and make good use of our strong points, only then will we be ready to decide on the course we want to embark on in life. There is no need whatsoever to be afraid of superiors, competitors, rivals, etc., as long as we know their true character and handle them accordingly. Granted that in some instances the only alternative will be to compromise in order to remain on good terms with many. However, we must reconcile ourselves to the fact that we cannot change human nature and, therefore, must accept people as they are.

Since nothing in this world is absolute, the evaluation of character traits, too, is relative. Character weaknesses which we often criticize, under certain circumstances can turn into assets. We know quite well that hypocrites, yes-men and opportunists quickly get into the good graces of people and have the advantage over many who cannot tacitly accede to the wishes of others.

As a matter of fact those of us who best measure up to certain requirements and by nature are endowed with basic traits and abilities indispensable for certain work, will best meet the demands of certain professions and occupations. There are many which often require harsh, callous, and even ruthless methods in which sentiments cannot play a part. According to the rule of the survival of the fittest, success does not always hinge on moral principles. In many instances, a man climbs to power much easier if he is tough-minded and cannot be swayed from his goal by feelings for humanity.

Men of success usually have an inborn knowledge of man. Due to their uncanny knowledge of human nature they can get along better with people and gain their ends with them because they handle them according to their nature. Would not everyone of you like to do the same simply by increasing your knowledge of man and thus, your chances of success?

There is a method to acquire extensive knowledge of self and also of others without personal contact with them, which eliminates the danger of being unduly influenced by likes and dislikes. It is the science of handwriting interpretation as demonstrated in this book.

This method of testing character can be of help to wives, mothers, husbands, fathers, adolescents, teachers, guardians, social workers, lawyers, judges, district attorneys, law enforcement agencies, clergymen, psychologists, psychiatrists, handwriting experts, businessmen, personnel directors, etc.

My personal experience with important business concerns taught me that this method can be used effectively to put the right man into the right place. Then the employee will not squander precious time in a position he is not suited for, and the employer will not spend money for inefficient personnel.

To the family this method of recognizing the nature of children will be beneficial. As a matter of fact, very few parents really know their offspring and often fool themselves by attributing flawless characters to them. On the other hand, they are often too critical in evaluating their children.

Much depends on the guidance and treatment a child is accorded in early life. If they are not brought up properly, if they are not taught to cope with and compensate for their shortcomings, if they are not treated according to their nature, as adolescents and adults, they will be bitter and hateful and join the army of wrong doers.

Psychologists, teachers, guardians and social workers, counselors can be enlightened about children and adults alike. By getting a realistic portrait of them, they can handle them more effectively and help them strengthen their morale.

How many frustrating and bitter experiences, how much strife and dissension could be avoided if we knew beforehand what to expect from a marriage partner, a business associate, a friend, etc.

Since the day I discovered my vocation for handwriting analysis, I have worked on the development of an authentic and exact method for the purpose of truthful and impartial character delineation.

My method not only reveals the true nature of a writer but also the impression a person conveys on and his attitude toward his world, how others see him and what they can expect of him. As a result of applying this method, the student will be prepared to deal with many persons with whom he would have frictions otherwise.

Because in my system the features can be identified without ambiguity, the student will have little difficulty in applying this method.

Even though not familiar with psychological disciplines, he can benefit from this system in many ways because the interpretations of my features are based on psychological terms.

With my method no intuition is needed. However, accurate observation of even the smallest, minutest details in a single letter of the alphabet is a must and this alone is a guarantee against the possibility of error in interpretation. The effectiveness of my method is limited only by a student's ability to write and to compare single letters of the alphabet with the deviations as they appear in handwriting.

I have dedicated forty years of my life to this work. If this approach to handwriting analysis is generally accepted and contributes toward better understanding between people, greater tolerance, greater consideration and a greater respect for the individuality of a person, I shall feel that my painstaking work will not have been in vain.

ARTHUR G. HOLT

CONTENTS

Chapter   *Page*

HANDWRITING IN
PSYCHOLOGICAL
INTERPRETATIONS

Chapter 1

HANDWRITING IDENTIFICATION AND INTERPRETATION

Two different professions use handwriting as a basis for their investigation. The first is called handwriting identification. The experts in this field are mostly employed by law enforcement agencies and lawcourts. Their work involves the examination of questioned documents. They identify a writer of a poison pen letter or a forger of a document by detecting subtle details and characteristic letter variations that are strictly personal and belong to a certain writer only.

In the field of suspect handwritings in America examiners accept the scientific fact that it is nearly impossible for any person to change or disguise his own handwriting for any length of time and that he will always fall back into his individual way of writing.

With the knowledge of my methodology, which essentially describes minute graphic details, practitioners could so enlarge their observations that their testimonial would increase in value. Handwriting experts could also use this method successfully by analyzing anonymous writers and by discovering specific character traits, which in many cases would make the search for the culprit easier for the authorities. In the courts such a graphological opinion could benefit judges, district attorneys, and defense attorneys by furnishing them with an insight into the oftimes complex nature of a defendant.

In Civil Court cases graphology can be of value when and where there is need for objective information about a person's character.

The second profession which concerns itself with the investigation of handwriting, is called handwriting interpretation or graphology. This book deals solely with the study of man's character and personality in handwriting.

Chapter 2

THE SCIENCE OF GRAPHOLOGY AND THE UNDERLYING THEORY OF THIS NEW APPROACH

One hundred years ago a French priest, Abbe Jean Hippolyte Michon, founded the science of graphology. After collecting handwritings at random, he determined that in every feature of writing a definite trait of character is revealed which can be attributed to the writer. The gestures he perceived in handwriting he called "jagged as lightning," "thread-like," "harpoon-shaped," "coiled," "snake-like," "saber-like," "spider-like," etc. For describing a person's character he used such terms as "cold," "hard," "rough," "unpleasant," "bizarre," "lilliputian," "exaggerated," "feminine," "masculine," "moderate," "harmonious," etc.

When he found it impossible to find a specific characteristic, he created the so-called "sign negative," and came to the conclusion that when, for instance, a handwriting showed no signs of courage and energy, the writer must be timid.

He also created a so-called "sign complex." That is, from the presence of a group of specific characteristics he deduced a general characteristic. Although he was the first scientist who used pictorial names to describe his findings, his interpretations were conflicting and superficial and not differentiated enough to delineate an accurate character portrait of a person. The French school of graphology had many distinguished scientists.

Divergent from the French school, the German school of Graphology put the main emphasis upon the action of writing, the physiological study of the nature of handwriting and the psychological study of the writer.

It was William Thierry Preyer (1895) who coined the term "brain writing" for handwriting by proving that writing is a function of the brain and that the arm and the hand are nothing but levers which carry out the movements of the pen, dictated by the brain. Through scientific experiments he deduced that writing is an expressive movement, one form of expression such as gestures, gait, posture, and facial expression.

The most prominent scholar of the German school is Ludwig Klages (1923) who retained in his work everything worth knowing which has been discovered in graphology up-to-date and which could rightly be considered as scientific research. He has proved that in the individual writing movements the character of the writer appears, and while writing he projects his innermost thoughts, feelings, and intentions, independent of the context of the text.

Klages accepts the theory that the special meaning of a feature in handwriting changes in each case and that any one characteristic feature may have one of several meanings, a positive or a negative. For instance, it may indicate a spirit of enterprise in one case, indolence in another, a lie in one case, diplomacy in another, depending on the form-level of the handwriting, on the rythmic beat which must not be mistaken for the aesthetic element in handwriting. Where there is rhythm, there is vitality and depth. With this theory Klages accepted the rhythm to be the primitive phenomenon of life and the standard of value in the interpretation of handwriting.

The correct interpretation of handwriting, Klages claims, is not an objective procedure in keeping with the principles of exact methods. The subjective personality of the analyst is the decisive factor. All depends on his faculty of forming a person's character portrait.

Since then many renowned European scholars have done research work and sought empirical and experimental validation of graphological theories. As a matter of fact, many West German and French universities include graphology in the clinical or applied psychology curriculum. Only recently, under the auspices of the Swiss Government, Zurich, a seminary opened its doors to the exclusive study of graphology.

In America many research materials are available but very few are written in textbook form. Since 1939, many psychologists and psychiatrists discussed the methodology and technique of graphological analysis. However, they were not trained graphologists.

For many years Klara G. Roman taught graphology at the New School for Social Research, New York. Her close collaborator Daniel S. Anthony, in his fight for the recognition of scientific graphology in America, wrote a chapter on this subject in a book entitled *Taboo Topics* (1963) to stimulate research, investigation and inquiry in those universities which major in projective techniques and the science of expressive movements of which graphology is probably the oldest method.

In my new approach to handwriting interpretation I incorporate two scientific principles, analysis and synthesis. Systematic and precise recording of minute details in and the general impression from handwriting must complement each other to claim the title "scientific." Like all human beings, those who specialize in graphology, likewise, have a different approach toward and outlook on life. Relatively few persons only are endowed with intuitive power, most of them proceed rationally and/or analytically. They all will be able to employ and apply this method. It establishes definite rules for numerous and hitherto imponderable graphic variables and concerns itself with their psychological interpretation.

For the first time in the history of graphology this new approach uses pictorial names for a great variety of letter-form variants, as they appear frequently and repeatedly in handwritings of different persons.

Since in a person there is a great discrepancy between reality and pretense, one of the most delicate tasks confronting the graphologist is to detect man's true nature. No doubt, the habit of wearing a mask is a human character trait and can be considered a must in his endeavor of adjusting himself to society. Society expects him to play his role in life as cleverly as possible. No wonder that anyone who wants to be a success, is forced to conform to these rules. The graphologist must answer the question whether man's liking for masquerade has become a habit or whether he uses a mask as a temporary means of self-protection.

In my new approach to handwriting interpretation I have taken pains of clearing away the ambiguities in the interpretation to relieve the analyst of some of the responsibility he has been burdened with in the past.

To avoid describing a person in terms of generalization, I generally give the interpretations in great detail and the characteristics are distinctly differentiated. Every single interpretation definitely explains a writer's individual thoughts, feelings, and intentions.

Not only have I emphasized basic character traits and marked tendencies but I have also interpreted repressed emotions. They reveal a writer's state of mind at different times and offer the possibility of analyzing specimens of handwriting written by the same person at different periods.

As a matter of fact errors in interpretation can occur only if the analyst is not sufficiently trained to observe the tiniest details in handwriting and to remember the wide variety of examples, each representing a description explaining how each illustration is formed and the name it bears, if any.

I have given a great part of the illustrations simple names derived from daily life, to facilitate the procedure of recognizing and remembering them.

I have integrated a great variety of the tiniest motions into the illustrations. I have incorporated size, dimension, proportion, angle, alignment, spacing, length, width, height, etc., in virtually each graphic illustration.

By explaining in slow motion how a writer deviates from the Latin alphabet he actually uses and arrives at his individual letter forms, I minutely describe the illustration which should be like the conforming picture in handwriting. The slightest deviation from it can lead to a different example and consequently to a different interpretation.

i.e., when the downstrokes below the line are curved concavely:

26

the writer has little power of resistance to temptation.

i.e., when the downstrokes below the line are curved convexly:

27

the writer extricates himself from situations which burden him with too much responsibility.

Since there are many facets of human nature and there are many ways and means for a person to veil the truth, I have incorporated a great variety of illustrations for the same or similar characteristics. If a certain character trait does not appear through a specific illustration, the writer may still possess it but may express the same characteristic in a different way, through a different illustration.

If ruthlessness appears frequently through various features in the

386  417

same handwriting, it is undoubtedly a prominent character trait of the writer.

A single characteristic feature in a handwriting standing by itself can be taken as a basis of analysis and must not be regarded in conjunction with any other feature. However, it is the sum total of all the features with their psychological interpretation which produces a complete character portrait of a person.

Chapter 3

PREREQUISITES TO THE STUDY
OF MY METHOD

We learn to write the alphabet according to a definite pattern. In spite of the Grade School teacher's endeavor to urge a pupil to copy the characters exactly in form, size, dimension, proportion, slant, alignment, spacing, etc., youngsters at an early age violate the rules of writing. And it is with these apparently insignificant deviations from the school pattern, which are already obvious in a first or second grader, that we must become acquainted. They clearly indicate the youngster's personality. They are the signposts by which we can direct him toward expressing his true individuality.

To familiarize ourselves with a writer's individual letter formations, we must get acquainted with the description above the illustration, which explains step-by-step how a certain writer forms his individual letter or letters and how they deviate from the standard of domestic and foreign alphabets.

In order to get acquainted with the terms used in the description of the examples in Chart I, let us have a good mental image of the formation of a single letter of the alphabet. Let us know how it starts and ends. Let us know its strokes, curves, loops, angles, etc., by their name and direction. On Chart I, No. 29, we will find that a hump is a convex stroke at the top of an upstroke and a downstroke.

29

As a ready reference for the names most of the examples bear, and as a specific reference for the letters of the alphabet in which they most frequently appear, and in which we most frequently may identify them, read the classified Index of Deviations from the Standard and their Names by numbers and letters, page 253, i.e., we will find an Auto Gearshift on No. 199 in the letter "d".

199

In the description, the number in parenthesis, which is close to the letter of the alphabet the writer presumably used, corresponds with the number below the letter of the domestic or Foreign alphabets on Chart II (Chapter 4, page 13), i.e., the description of example No. 250

250

depicts the Foreign f (8)

but basically any long letter "f" in the standard could have been considered for determining the slightest deviations.

If the cursive f (7)

would have been depicted, the description would be as follows:

When the cursive f (7) has no lower loop and the downstroke narrows to a point below the line.

CHART I

TERMS USED IN THE DESCRIPTION OF THE EXAMPLES
(Arrows show direction)

1    curve concave,
vertical
hollowed to the right

2    curve convex,
vertical
hollowed to the left

3    curve concave,
horizontal
hollowed above

4    curve convex,
horizontal
hollowed below

5    downstroke straight,
ends in a point
at the baseline

6    downstroke double-curved,
indicates the end of the
first part of the letter

7
downstroke (curve)
convex
ends at the baseline

8    downstroke (curve)
concave
ends at the baseline

9 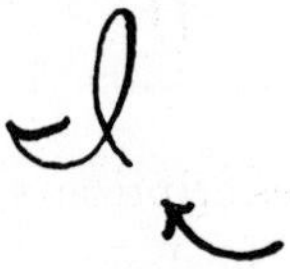   upstroke (upcurve) of the loop
concave
begins at the baseline

10    upstroke (upcurve)
convex
begins at the baseline

11    initial stroke (curve)
left tending, convex,
horizontal; final curve
(stroke) left tending,
concave, horizontal

12
letter parts
above and below the line

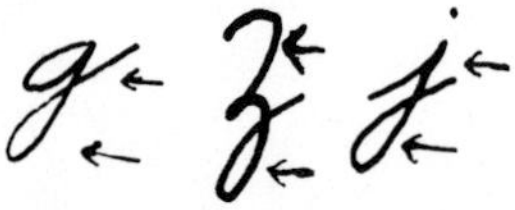

13    downstroke (curve)
concave
vertical

14    half circle
convex
vertical

15    stroke (curve)
left tending,
convex
upward slanting

16 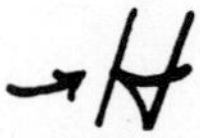   final stroke (curve)
right tending,
concave
horizontal

17 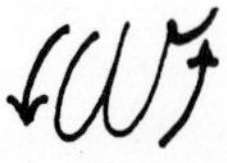   initial downstroke (curve)
concave; final downstroke
(curve) convex

18    initial upstroke (curve)
right tending, concave;
final upstroke (curve)
right tending, convex

19    final upstroke (curve)
convex; ends at the
left side of the down-
stroke and curves back
to the baseline

CHART I (cont.)

20

the crossing of the upper loop is high

21

the crossing of the upper loop is low

22

back of an upper loop followed by the down-stroke below the loop ending in a point at the baseline

23

downstroke below the line and upstroke of the lower loop

24

indirect loop slants in a different direction than the following downstroke

25

back of the direct loop slants in the same direction as the downstroke of the second part of the letter

26

direct oval (arc) begins counter clockwise

27

indirect arc begins clockwise forming the second part of the letter

28

final downstroke ending in a point below the line

29

a hump is a convex stroke at the top of an upstroke and a downstroke

30

slant line forming an angle with the following concave downcurve

31

upstroke retraces the preceding downstroke below and above the line

32

downstroke retraces the preceding upstroke

33

tick- and tick-out strokes

34

intermediate stroke connects two downstrokes and partly retraces the preceding downstroke

35

connecting lines consist of the final stroke of the preceding letter and the initial stroke of the following letter

Chapter 4

STANDARD LETTERS OF DOMESTIC
AND FOREIGN ALPHABETS

CHART II

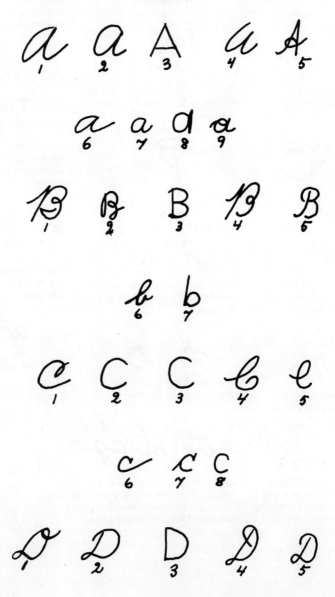

CHART II (cont.)

CHART II (cont.)

CHART II (cont.)

CHART II (cont.)

CHART II (cont.)

CHART II (cont.)

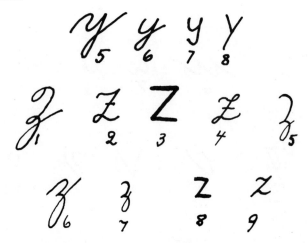

Standard numbers, fractions, signs, and punctuation marks

Chapter 5

A WRITER'S INTELLECTUAL
STANDARD AND IMAGINATIVE POWER

To determine the intellectual standard and imaginative power of a writer is a matter of practice and experience and can be done by anyone with the help of the following samples and suggestions. The more a writer's letter forms deviate from the school pattern by simplification, ornamentation and originality, the more intelligent and or artistic is he.

Sample No. I reveals a writer whose letters do not deviate much from the school pattern. He is of average intelligence only, has few mental interests and few original ideas.

We eat dinner at six o'clock

I

Try not to make any more error

Samples No. II and III can be classified among writers whose letter forms are simplified to a certain extent but lack individual ornamentation. They possess enough natural intelligence to grasp and understand ordinary matters. Their interest is centered mainly around practical and tangible subjects.

II

with you so often last winter

and spring and not at all this

III

time I will write as

work were to be published

Sample No. IV reveals a writer whose capitals are intertwined and adorned with strokes and flourishes which do not belong to them. Such a person is endowed with shrewd intelligence. He can convince others of his own importance by boasting, bragging, and showing off.

IV

Samples No. V and VI are those of intelligent persons with a standard far above average. Although their letter forms are simplified, they show originality and there are no unnecessary ornamentations or elaborations. These writers have the ability to judge matters critically and to promote useful ideas.

V

Your publicity in Life magazine and many other publications must

VI

If you can reach some Conclusion from this jumbled

Samples No. VII, VIII and IX reveal writers who are both keenly intelligent and artistic. Their letters show esthetical and ornamental forms that seem to be almost three dimensional and indicate their artistic leanings and interests, their excellent taste and creative ideas. They differ from the previously shown rather prosaic writers because of their imaginative power.

VII

lover   Easter   father

Gabriele   Jerry

VIII

This is just to wish you a
1941 and to thank you for

IX

tween the Two   you may
is sufficient material on
will to base the analys
Question.

Chapter 6

SIMPLE DEVIATIONS FROM COPYBOOK MODELS AND THEIR RECOGNITION

One of the rules we were taught in school is that five letters are about three times the size of the small letters which are one space high. These are the tall and long letters "b," "f," "h," "k," "l." Capital letters are the same size as the tall letters. The three letters "d," "p," "t" are a little shorter, two-thirds of the space of the tall letters. The letter parts below the line extend about two-thirds of the space.

Another rule is uniform height of all short, tall, long and capital letters and of all letter parts below the line. To recognize letters of equal length above or below the line, compare two letters "dd," "ff," "ll," "tt," "fl," "fh," "gg," "yy," "pp," "py," "fg," "gy," "jp," etc.

When these rules are observed, the writer deliberates before acting and acts in accordance with an opinion once formed.

When tall letters are unequal in length,

3   *test hack heal will*

the writer is not steadfast and can be induced to change his mind and reverse his attitude.

When tall letters and capitals are unequal in length,

4   *Continental Bldg*

the writer may compromise his principles and act against his own convictions.

When the loops and or strokes below the line are unequal in length,

5   *keep paying of your*

the writer when impelled by his instincts, can be influenced to compromise principles and unpredictable and irrational acts can be expected.

When the tall and/or long letters are of equal length above the line and the loops and/or strokes below the line are unequal in length,

6   *bufferin*   *by bishops*

the writer usually thinks consistently and will not easily be influenced to change his course. However, when impelled by his instincts, he can be influenced to compromise principles and act irrationally.

When capital letters are much longer in proportion to the small letters,

7   *Eagle Rose*

the writer assumes an air of superiority in order to hide his lack of self-confidence.

When the loops and/or strokes below the line are too long in proportion to the letters and/or letter parts above the line,

8

the writer yields to his strong appetites and desires.

When several "f's" show different sizes,

9

the writer's moods change unexpectedly. He can be enthusiastic one moment and lose interest the next.

When the printed capitals are gradually reduced at the top,

10

the writer is apt to change his course and attitude according to the benefit he hopes to gain.

When the size of printed capitals increases towards the end,

11

N · Y · C

the writer has the tendency to force his will upon others.

When the size of printed capitals gradually decreases and increases at the top so that a half circle can be drawn over the letters,

12

the writer is mainly concerned about safeguarding his own interests and acts according to expedience.

When small letters get smaller in perspective towards the end of a word,

13   *Recommand*

the writer keeps people at a distance in order to maintain an unbiased viewpoint and an objective attitude towards them.

When the tall letters and capitals have almost the same size as the small letters,

14   *United States of amerika*

the writer's most desired goal is to protect his own interests and others are important only when he can use them.

When the downstroke of the "t" is exceptionally low and the bar touches it, crosses it at the top or is above it,

15   *battle   in*

the writer is concerned about his own well-being and does nothing without a selfish purpose in mind.

When the first small letter is much larger than the following small letters,

16   *lua   sta*

the writer is of a domineering nature.

When the letter "a" shows striking differences in size,

17   *a   a   a   a   a*

the writer has times when his self-confidence is so low that his initiative and enthusiasm weaken.

When there are striking differences in the size of the small letters "m," "n," "o" written on the baseline,

18 *Condition: do some men working*

the writer's actions depend on whether he is attracted or repelled by people. If he is attracted, they can take advantage of him, but if he is repelled, he will take advantage of them.

When there are striking differences in the size of the letter "o",

19 *Oblong   robot   overlook*

the writer has times when he acts too impulsively so that he may overlook important details. At other times he acts too cautiously and thus may miss chances.

When in several letters "m" and/or "n" the downstrokes are pointed at the top and round at the bottom alternative with others which conform to the rule,

20   *uau   man*

or when in several letters "m" and/or "n" the last down stroke is pointed at the top,

20a   *man*

the writer is wavering, apt to abandon his opinion, and reverse his attitude unexpectedly.

When in capitals the downstrokes, and in tall letters the downstrokes and the backs of the loops are straight,

21   *Pa   Bob   had*
     like   the   Ry

the writer possesses the necessary willpower and stamina to translate ideas into action.

When the cursive f (7) is loopless; and when the downstroke is straight, vertical, or almost vertical, and ends in a point below the line,

22   *f*

the writer can be aloof and reserved.

When the downstrokes of tall letters and/or capitals are curved concavely,

23

the writer tends to acquiesce and agree with those from whom he hopes to gain.

When the downstrokes of tall letters are curved concavely and convexly alternately,

24

the writer is very flexible in the way he adapts himself to people and situations and will compromise at the opportune moment if he hopes to benefit.

When the downstrokes of tall letters and/or capitals and/or the backs of the loops are wavy,

25

the writer lacks backbone and stamina and is wavering in conduct and purpose.

When downstrokes below the line are curved concavely,

26

the writer has little power of resistance to temptation.

When downstrokes below the line are curved convexly,

27

the writer extricates himself from situations which burden him with too much responsibility.

When the upper loop of the "f" is pointed or when, instead of the loop, the downstroke retraces the initial upstroke to an extent,

28

the writer is stubborn and will listen to no one.

When the loops in capitals and tall letters or in long letters above the line are very wide,

29

the writer is a show off and inclined to present himself in the best possible light.

When the loops below the line show every and any type of variation,

30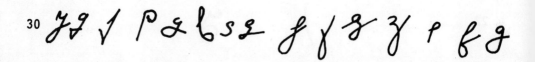

the writer can be so changeable in his behavior and becomes so unpredictable that all sorts of surprises can be expected.

Chapter 7

THE SLANT OF THE WRITING

As a rule all downstrokes must be parallel and uniformly slanted, either slightly to the right,

31

or vertically,

32

if these rules are observed, the writer's veracity cannot be questioned.

When tall letters and capitals and long letters slant to the left (backhand writing),

33

the writer resorts to dissimulation and maneuvers as the easiest way out of disagreeable and embarrassing situations.

When tall letters and capitals and long letters slant far to the right,

34

the writer seeks to place himself in the best light to prevent others from detecting his imperfections.

When in a backhand writing a capital letter slants to the right,

35

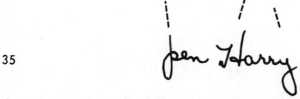

the writer is not trustworthy and may betray confidences.

When in a word the first letter, which has a part below the line, slants to the right, and when one of the following letters, which have a part below the line, slant to the left so if lines are drawn through them they meet above the line,

36

or when the tall letters and/or capitals in a word slant to the right and one of the following letters, which have a part below the line, slants to the left so that if lines are drawn through them they meet above the line,

37

the writer resorts to skillful maneuvers as the easiest way out of disagreeable and embarrassing situations so that it will be difficult to figure him out.

When in a word the downstrokes of a single "m" and/or "n" slant to the left, while the tall letters slant to the right,

38

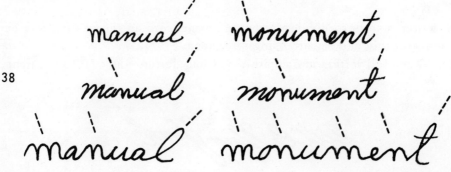

the writer can say the opposite of what he really means so subtly and unnoticeably and sound so convincing that no one suspects him of deceit.

When the first letters of a word slant to the right while the following slant to the left,

39

the writer in general tells the truth but will distort it when he thinks to profit.

When the letter "t" or a capital letter at the beginning of a word slopes to the right and another "t" slopes to the left at the end of a word so if lines are drawn through them they meet above the line,

40

the writer has the tendency to boast, brag, and to color the truth.

When small letters, long letters, capitals and letter parts below the line slant in different directions,

41

the writer's vivid imagination makes it difficult for him to distinguish between truth and fiction. He believes in things in which he wants to believe.

When the last downstroke of one or more "m" or "n" slants to the left,

42

the writer uses white lies to back out of a difficulty.

When the last downstroke of one or more "m's" or "n's" does not reach the baseline and slants to the left,

43

the writer can slyly extricate himself from unwelcome situations.

When the downstroke of one or more "r's" in a word slants to the left, while other small letters slope to the right,

44

the writer does not take the responsibility for faults and is prone to place the blame on others.

When the first downstroke of the printed "N" slants to the right, the second downstroke is vertical and the center stroke slants to the left,

45   N

the writer has the tendency to misrepresent facts and finds it difficult to distinguish between truth and fiction.

When the downstroke of one or more "i's" in a word slants to the left, while other small letters slope to the right,

46   *Mining   his*

the writer has a limited sense of loyalty.

When two "o's" or an o-oval and a d-oval follow each other but have different slants,

47   *oa   od*

the writer pretends not to notice the intentions of others but is well aware of what is on their mind and cannot easily be fooled.

When one or more ''o's'' slant to the left while other small letters slope to the right,

48   *Role*   *Monitor*

the writer has the tendency to conceal his real thoughts, feelings, and intentions.

Chapter 8

THE I-DOTS

When the i-dot is in line with the downstroke and at level with the t-bar,

49   *its*   *cities*

the writer knows his own mind and makes his own decisions.

When the i-dots, which may be short downward slanting lines, are higher than the rule stipulates but in line with the downstroke,

50   *it*   *ti*

the writer is distracted and forgetful.

When the i-dots are made at the left side of the downstroke,

51   *in it*

the writer practices great caution in order to avoid making mistakes and not to miss changes.

When the i-dots are made at the right side of the downstroke,

52   *in it*

the writer has the strong desire to be active and enterprising.

When the i-dots are made at the left and at the right side of the downstroke, alternately,

53   *will it*

the writer has the strong desire to be active and enterprising but at times is at odds with himself and does not see things and situations clearly to go ahead.

When the i-dots, which are short lines, straight or curved, slant to the left and are close to the downstroke of the printed "i" or "j,"

54   *inhis   l·y   is*

the writer feigns warm feelings for others so that they believe him ready to sacrifice.

When the i-dots are short lines and slant in different directions,

55   *in in hild ming*

the writer is subject to contradictory emotions so that he is unpredictable in his actions and attitudes.

When the i-dots consist of a period and a curve or of a short and a longer line forming an angle,

56   *1 ti' i im*

the writer is very domineering, can force others to comply with his wishes and has the tendency to degrade and humiliate them.

When the i-dots show every and any type of variation, position and direction,

57   *ehhion it ride in
        in is it in is it*

the writer is apt to change his attitude and course frequently and goes from one extreme to the other so that uniformity and consistency cannot be expected of him.

When the i-dots consist of two curved lines which join or cross

58   *l   i*

the writer makes offers and propositions which by clever tricks he may disavow later.

When the i-dots are heavy and resemble a rectangle,

59

ı

the writer would not hesitate to resort to harsh measures.

Chapter 9

PUNCTUATION MARKS—
WORDS UNDERLINED

When the two periods of the colon (g) which are short vertical lines, are followed by a dash,

60   *red ; -*   *fer ; —*

the writer behind a mask of affability conceals his inner self and also his true feelings towards others.

When commas (g), curved or straight, are longer than one-half of the height of the small letters,

61   *her)*   *Love ,*

the writer is very sensitive and his feelings are easily hurt.

When the dashes (g) are unusually long,

62   *one___*

the writer at times can be so aloof, icy, and reserved that others are kept at a distance.

When the dashes (g) have a double curve,

63   *it ⌒___*

the writer has the power both to convince and impress people.

When the period of the exclamation mark (g) is directly below the downstroke,

64   !

the writer knows exactly what he wants and acts accordingly.

When the period of the exclamation mark (g) is at the right side of the downstroke,

65   !.

the writer adopts a wait-and-see attitude in order not to forfeit chances.

When the period of the exclamation mark (g) is at the left side of the downstroke,

66   .!

the writer has initiative and drive.

When the periods of the exclamation marks (g) are made at the left and at the right side of the downstroke, alternately,

67   !   !

the writer has a strong desire to be active and enterprising but at times is at odds with himself and does not see things and situations clearly to go ahead.

When a word is underlined with a stroke parallel to it and a good distance off,

68   CPD

the writer can make everything he presents appealing and attractive.

When a word is underlined twice,

69   recommend

the writer by giving himself an air of importance, wants to impress his world.

When a word is underlined with a double curve,

70   Via Air Mail

the writer has the power both to convince and impress people.

Chapter 10

PECULIARITIES IN PEN-PRESSURE

When the pen-pressure is uniformly light,

71

> *You may a
> uth brotherhooc
> has created*

the writer is undecided, wavering, not steady in purpose and refuses to take a firm stand.

When the pen-pressure results in pasty writing,

72

> *ulf Coastal
> of the most*

the writer's salacious imagination has a direct bearing on his outlook and conduct.

When the downstrokes of long letters or letters below the line are heavily inked, but their upstrokes much lighter,

73

the writer can control people.

When the letters are heavier inked above the line but much lighter below the line,

74

fat

the writer lacks drive and stamina.

When the pen-pressure in small letters is heavier than in the rest,

75   *would be a four and for a final mark*

the writer has a good sense of values but lacks the initiative necessary for innovational changes.

When the stroke below the line is heavily inked at the end,

76   *y*

the writer has a choleric temper.

CONNECTIONS AND SEPARATIONS

When the connecting lines between letters are unequal in length,

Andrea   June

77

coperation   Crescent

the writer's internal conflicts often induce him to become impatient and intolerant.

When connecting lines and/or intermediate strokes are almost horizontal and straight on the baseline,

Coming   and

78

Naaman   Sincere

the writer conveys the impression of being self-controlled, calm and composed.

When the incomplete oval of the cursive o (5) or the final upstroke of the cursive w (6) has no tick-out stroke and directly curves into the first downstroke of the following cursive n (6) or into the downstroke of the following cursive r (8) or i (6) ending in a point,

79   *in*   *on*   *w*   *ir*   *wi*

the writer due to his excellent sense of orientation, can grasp matters and adapt himself to people and situations so quickly and cleverly that he can handle any situation even though he is given little information.

When a cursive capital letter stands alone in a word in which the following letters are connected,

80   *Walter*

the writer has little patience and permits himself to be influenced by unimportant incidents to lose interest in people and matters.

When the cursive "e" is separated from the previous letter and begins with a short concave downstroke far above the baseline,

81   *tp*

or when the cursive "i" is separated from the following letter and the i-dot is connected with the following letter by a curved stroke,

82   *elz   ,5   light*

or when there is a break between the cursive "i" and the following letter,

83   *i'f   will*

the writer can become so disappointed with people that his suspicion is aroused.

When the connecting lines between small letters and between small letters and tall letters are about twice as long as the height of the small letters,

84   *who*

the writer carefully weighs, investigates, and examines matters before he arrives at a conclusion.

When the connecting line between the cursive letters "le" (6, 7), is short and either the preceding or the following connecting line is much longer,

85   *hle   ole   let*

the writer pretends to be conservative and a stickler to principles in order to escape embarrassing situations.

Chapter 12

THE ALIGNMENT OF LETTERS AND WORDS

When the letters of the first part of a word ascend, of the second part descend,

86

the writer has a remarkable flair telling him in a flash if matters, people or opportunities are valuable, suitable or useful.

When the first part or the first letter of a word is on the baseline and the second part or the following letters are higher,

87

or when the second or third hump of the letter "m" or the last hump of the letter "n" is higher than the previous,

88

the writer without much effort can cleverly adapt himself to all kinds of situations, never losing perspective and sight of his underlying purpose.

When the second part of a word drops below the baseline,

89

the writer at present is so much absorbed in his problems that he does not see people and situations clearly, a condition which adversely affects his actions.

When the last small letter of a word is definitely higher than the preceding small or tall letter,

90

the writer can easily make friends and win his way into the good graces of people.

When the letters in words are alternately above and below the baseline and are ascending and descending,

91   *the New York side I will outside of New York*

the writer is ruthless in pursuing his aims.

When the second of two consecutive "f's" is higher than the first one,

92   *ff*

the writer is so shrewd, cunning, and artfull that no matter what difficulty he gets into, he is always on the winning side.

When successive words are higher,

93   *I'm asking myself what is*

the writer is inwardly tense, a condition which adversely reflects on his courage so that he is not strong enough to wrestle with difficulties.

Chapter 13

INITIAL AND FINAL STROKES

When the initial upstrokes in a cursive script are missing,

94 *me in te pi he from will*

the writer can be cool, icy, and aloof.

When in a cursive script there are alternately initial upstrokes or none,

95 *pro was that vacaim mild*

the writer is apt to change his attitude. At times he can be cool, icy and aloof, at other times friendly, neighborly, and sympathetic.

When in tall letters, capitals, long letters or in letter parts above the line the initial stroke, which is high above the baseline, is long, concave and horizontal and may begin with a short, concave downcurve,

96

the writer's apparent willingness to oblige and help is a clever trick to win the acceptance and trust of others.

When in small letters, in letter parts above the line, in tall letters or in capitals, the initial upstroke begins with a short downcurve or with a hook above, on or below the baseline,

97

45

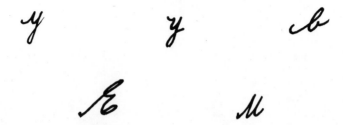

the writer tries to gain his ends by all sorts of tricks and ruses.

When a long, straight, or undercurved initial upstroke begins below the baseline,

98

the writer is ready to vex and humiliate anyone who dares to curtail his desire for independence.

When a concave initial upstroke begins with a short hook or curve below, on, or above the baseline,

99

the writer controls others by tricks and schemes.

When the final upstroke as in the cursive "r" is extremely long and has a double curve,

100

the writer can be very pleasant to make others believe that they have won his confidence, but when he has reached his objective, he may surreptitiously inflict injury.

When final strokes in small letters are long and make a left turn at the end,

101

the writer may agree to the propositions of others but will not live up to his obligations.

When final strokes, which may be concave, straight or convex, horizontal, or downward slanting, are long and more heavily inked towards the end,

102

the writer is unrestrained and apt to lose his temper.

When final strokes are long, horizontal and end with a hook or curve turned down,

103

the writer can become antagonistic and attack people in their vulnerable spots.

When the letter "e" ends with a loop; or when the final downstroke of the letter "l" or "d" ends abruptly before it reaches the baseline,

104

the writer can be easily hurt and takes such incidents so much to heart that he finds it difficult to forget them.

When a final stroke ends with a small, left tending, ink-filled loop,

105

the writer is insidious.

When certain tall or small letters end with a long, straight, horizontal stroke,

106

or when the final stroke of the letter "E" curves back to the baseline and crosses the horizontal curve,

107

the writer is reticent and keeps people at a distance.

When the final strokes of certain small letters which are long, straight, horizontal or slant upwards, narrow to a point,

108

or when the final stroke of the letter "f" narrows to a point,

109

the writer has the tendency to nag, needle, and criticize others and their actions.

When horizontal final strokes end in a short hook or curve turned up to the left,

110

the writer wants to have an easy life at the expense of others and slyly takes advantage of them.

Chapter 14

LETTERS OF THE ALPHABET RESEMBLING
PICTORIAL FORMS: LETTERS "A" AND "a"

Now we must concentrate on a great number of examples to which I have given names of nature and life not only because they resemble them but also to make it easier for us to remember them and to identify them in a handwriting.

We must not expect these pictorial forms to be perfect. In many instances they are nothing but fragmentary copies of the forms they represent. They are in alphabetical order.

They can appear in one letter, in a few letters of the alphabet and in all directions. Therefore, we must look at a specimen handwriting from all sides, from the front, from the left side, right side or upside down. An arrow indicates the direction in which the pictorial forms appear in this book. Many pictorial forms can be identified immediately without moving the page.

When in the Foreign A (5) the loop is very large and extends far beyond the left side of the initial upstroke,

111

this is a LOOP EXTENDING BEYOND THE LETTER and the writer cleverly hides malicious and perfidious designs.

When the incomplete oval of the cursive A (1) starts with a short, convex upcurve followed by the downcurve forming a narrow curve with a short, almost straight upstroke, and when the latter forms an angle with a short, straight, left tending downstroke ending in a narrow curve which has an upward slanting, concave, final stroke,

112

49

this is a HEAD OF A BIRD and the writer uses all sorts of maneuvers and schemes to intimidate people and make them accede to his will.

When the printed A (3) begins at the baseline and is partly round at the top, and when the upstroke is close to the downstroke and the bar is low,

113   *A*

this is an ELEPHANT'S TUSK and the writer feigns a sense of duty and dependability with ulterior motives.

When one or two downstrokes of printed capitals narrow to a point,

114   *A*

this is a STING OF A WASP and the writer is given to bickering and provokes, criticizes, and belittles others.

When in the printed A (3) after the first downstroke is made, the second downstroke is concave and longer at the bottom than the first one,

115   *A*

this is a DEFECTIVE STEP-LADDER and the writer pretends to be in need of advice and affection but is likely to bite the hand that feeds him.

When in the printed A (3) after the first downstroke is made, the second downstroke is convex and the bar touches or slightly crosses it,

116   *A*   *A*

these are SUN DIALS and the writer waits for an opportunity to retaliate.

When the first downstroke of the printed A (3) does not join the second one, and when the bar crosses the second downstroke and narrows to a point,

117   → *A*

this is a BRAD AWL and the writer is prone to discredit people by indulging in carping criticism.

When in the printed A (3) the bar is concave and crosses the two downstrokes or only one and touches the other,

118

these are MERIDIANS and the writer has the tendency to vex and humiliate others by passive resistance.

When the cursive A (1) begins above the baseline with a convex upcurve forming an angle with a straight downstroke which in turn forms an
angle with a short, final upcurve, and when the latter, which is close to
the initial upcurve, is slightly retraced by the final downstroke ending
above the baseline,

119

this is a WAXING MOON and the writer is apt to change his attitude unexpectedly and becomes sarcastic, caustic, and acrimonious.

When the cursive A (1), a (6), begins with a long, convex upcurve,
and when, after the downcurve is made, a short upcurve ends in an oblong,
ink-filled loop which does not touch the initial upcurve, and when the
final stroke joins the initial stroke,

120

these are RELIGIOUS MEDALS and the writer pretends to foster ideals
and virtues.

When in the cursive A (2) after the initial downcurve is made, the
short upcurve ends in a small loop, and when the second part of the following Foreign p (9) has a downcurve ending in a point which is slightly
retraced by a straight final stroke,

121

or when the cursive a (6) has a long final stroke which ends in a point
below the baseline, and when the second part of the following Foreign
p (9) has a downcurve ending in a point which is slightly retraced by a
straight final stroke,

122

these are the FRACTIONS 6/2 and 9/2, and the writer is very calculating and figures everything in dollars and cents before he takes any action.

When the oval of the cursive a (6) or printed a (8) is circular or elliptical, free of inner loops or strokes,

123   a a

these are CIRCLES AND/OR ELLIPSES and the writer has a zeal for work.

When the oval of the cursive a (6) is incomplete and has a small opening, and when the final upcurve is shorter than the downcurve and has an upward slanting tick-out stroke,

124   σ

this is an ACORN and the writer often does not know what he wants and is wavering in his decisions.

When the oval of the cursive a (6) or printed a (8) is almost in horizontal position,

125   α

this is a HORIZONTAL OVAL and the writer is a slow thinker, needs time before he makes up his mind, and is not very enterprising.

When the final downstroke of the cursive a (6) retraces the oval to and ends below the baseline,

126   a

or when the final downstroke of the cursive a (6, 7) which does not reach the baseline, turns in horizontal direction near the top,

127   a a α

these are PARASITES and the writer slyly takes advantage of people.

When the cursive a (6) consists of two "e's" of almost equal height which join and have flattened loops,

128   ee

these are INFANTS WITH FLATTENED HEADS and the writer can become headstrong and obstinate.

When the incomplete oval of the cursive a (6) ends in a small loop followed by the final downstroke which has a double curve and does not retrace the oval,

129

this is a BODY LEANING BACK and the writer through charm and affability seeks to profit from people.

When the initial stroke of the cursive a (6) is horizontal and starts above the baseline followed by a left slanting, indirect loop touching the baseline, and when a concave upstroke joins the complete "a" which slants to the right and touches the preceding loop,

130

or when the cursive a (6) consists of two "e's" of different form and size which join, and when the second "e" does not reach the baseline,

131

these are CUNNING EYES and the writer can adapt himself to others so adroitly that they think he is highly interested in them and take his words at face value, while in reality he has mental reservations.

When the oval of the cursive a (6, 7) begins with a convex upcurve, which is made within the oval, and when the rest of the letter does not reach the baseline,

132

these are DREAMY EYES and the writer knows how to evoke the good will of others and to win their acceptance.

When the cursive a (6) begins at the baseline with an undercurved upstroke followed by the downcurve of the oval ending in an ink-filled loop inside the oval,

133

this is an EVASIVE EYE and the writer would not hesitate to be deceitful and disloyal if his own interests were at stake.

When the cursive a (6) begins with a short, convex upcurve followed by the downcurve and the short upcurve of the oval, which ends in an oblong ink-filled loop joining the starting point of the letter,

134

this is the EVIL EYE and the writer can deliberately make life difficult for others.

When in the cursive a (7), after the downcurve is made, the upcurve comes to a stop before the oval is completed and forms an angle with the final downstroke within the oval which is straight, very close to the up-curve, and ends in a point,

135

this is an EYE-LID CAST DOWN and the writer makes a guileless and naive impression as if he could be taken advantage of.

When the oval of the cursive a (6, 7) is incomplete, ends with an "l-" or "e-loop" within the oval which does not reach the baseline,

136

these are IRRESISTIBLE EYES and the writer exerts a fascinating in-fluence on people and can win their affection, acceptance, and confidence.

When the cursive a (7) begins with a short upcurve followed by the downcurve, and when the final upcurve has a loop at the end which is half in and half outside the oval,

137

these are POPPING EYES and the writer conceals his selfish intentions by pretending to be both interested and sympathetic.

When the oval of the cursive a (7) begins with a period within the oval and a short, convex upcurve followed by the initial downcurve and a short, final upcurve which joins the initial upcurve, and when the final downstroke is almost eliminated,

138

this is a SPARKLING EYE and the writer tries to get himself into the good graces of others by being so fascinating and alluring that he can control them.

When the initial downcurve of the cursive a (6) forms a narrow curve with, and is much longer than the following upcurve, and when the final downstroke partly retraces the upcurve and turns to the right before it reaches the baseline,

139

these are AUTHORITATIVE FINGERS and the writer has the tendency to browbeat and humiliate others.

When the cursive a (6, 7) starts with an initial upstroke followed by a short, straight, left slanting downstroke and a short, straight, right slanting upstroke which form angles around which the oval is drawn,

140

this is an EMBLEM OF A SECRET ALLIANCE and the writer assumes the appearance of loyalty and integrity to win the confidence of people and induce them to discard their reserve.

When the oval of the cursive a (6, 7) or Foreign a (9) forms a narrow curve at the bottom and closes with a loop within the oval, and when the final stroke does not reach the baseline,

141

this is a QUIVER and the writer is bitterly vindictive.

When the cursive a (6, 7) consists of a straight, left tending upstroke forming an angle with the straight, initial downstroke, and when the downstroke in turn forms an angle with the straight, final upstroke, which joins the initial stroke, and when the rest of the letter which is higher, joins the preceding part at the starting point,

142

this is a SMALL HATCHET and the writer, when his feelings are hurt, will seek revenge.

When in the cursive a (7) the incomplete oval begins with a slightly convex upstroke forming an oblong, pointed loop with the downcurve longer than the rest of the letter,

143

this is the FIRST QUARTER OF THE MOON and the writer conceals his tendency to dominate behind apparent kindness and humility.

When the cursive a (6, 7) begins with a long, convex upstroke ending in a large loop followed by a final stroke, which turns to the right at the point where the crossing ends and almost slants in the same direction as the initial upstroke,

144

or when the cursive a (6, 7) starts with a long, horizontal or upward slanting stroke which ends in an oversized loop, and when the final downstroke is greatly reduced at the top followed by the final upstroke which slants almost in the same direction as the initial upstroke,

145

these are STONES and the writer can make difficulties for others and put obstacles in their way so furtively that he cannot easily be held responsible.

When in the cursive a (6, 7) after the downcurve is made, the upcurve of the incomplete oval ends in a loop which may or may not have a final stroke,

146

this is the NUMBER 6 and the writer craves money and possessions so intensely that he would do anything in his power to acquire them.

When the cursive a (6) is connected with an oval of the cursive d (6) which stands alone and is higher than the preceding letter, and when the two ovals are shaped differently,

147

or when the two ovals of the cursive ag (7, 8) are shaped differently, and when the connecting line is longer than the height of the ovals and forms a concave horizontal curve at the baseline,

148

these are UNUSABLE EYE GLASSES AND LORGNETTES and the writer
is inquisitive, enjoys detecting the weak spots in others, and gossiping
about them.

When the cursive a (7) begins with an almost straight upstroke
above the baseline followed by the initial downcurve which crosses the
preceding upstroke, and when after the final upcurve is made, the final
downstroke is short and does not reach the baseline, and when a long,
upward slanting connecting line joins the next cursive l (6) which is
higher than the preceding letter and has a horizontal final stroke,

149

this is a RAILWAY TRAFFIC SIGNAL and the writer gives himself an air
of importance by directing and guiding others and assuming the guise of
a responsible and reliable person.

When a word begins with the cursive a (6, 7), and when after the
oval is made, the short, left slanting, final downstroke does not reach the
baseline, and when the downstrokes of the following m, n (6), which are
not retraced and slope to the left, are partly round at the top and at the
bottom, and gradually shorter towards the end, and when the final stroke
is horizontal,

150

these are DRILLS and the writer will make every effort to accomplish his
goal even if bulldog tenacity and force are required.

When a word begins with the cursive a (6), and when after the oval
is made, the short, left slanting, final downstroke does not reach the baseline, and when the downstrokes of the following cursive m (6), which are
not retraced and slope to the left, are partly round at the top and at the
bottom and gradually shorter towards the end, and when the final stroke
joins the succeeding cursive o (5) almost in the center,

151

this is an UNUSUAL DRILL and the writer in spite of his efforts to attain
a goal, often fails because he has no real system and wastes energy.

When the final downstroke of the cursive a (6) is reduced at the top and does not reach the baseline, and when a connecting line which is longer than the height of the preceding and following letter, curves into the convex downstroke of the cursive s (8),

152

this is a DOUBLE HOOK and the writer grasps every opportunity to succeed even at the expense of others.

When in the cursive a (6, 7) after the oval is made, which may or may not be complete, the last downstroke is reduced at the top and does not reach the baseline, and when a connecting line joins the concave downstroke of the following cursive t (5) which ends below the baseline and slants in a different direction than the preceding "a," and when the bar, if any, does not cross the downstroke,

153

these are LAMPS WITH A GOOSE NECK and the writer feigns warm feelings for others so that they believe him ready to sacrifice.

Chapter 15

LETTERS OF THE ALPHABET RESEMBLING PICTORIAL FORMS: LETTERS "B" AND "b"

When the cursive B (1) begins with a straight upstroke followed by a short downstroke and a long, left tending upcurve which turns to the right, widens at the end, and curves into the upper indirect arc, and when the lower indirect arc slightly retraces the upper one,

154

or when the cursive B (1) begins with a short downstroke followed by a retrace stroke and a much longer and decidedly right slanting upcurve which joins the first indirect arc, and when the second indirect arc slightly retraces the first one and joins the initial upcurve at the starting point,

155

these are HEARTS and the writer gives the impression of being whole-heartedly interested in others, and concentrating all his efforts on their behalf . . . a clever maneuver on his part which helps him to win their trust.

When the printed B (3) begins with a straight upstroke followed by the upper indirect arc which is connected with the lower one by a concave curve, and when the latter does not join the initial stroke,

156

these are ORNAMENTAL STONE COFFINS and the writer pretends to be able to keep a secret so that people trust him and are only too glad to give him information which they otherwise would have kept to themselves.

When in the cursive B (1) after the initial downstroke is made, an upcurve follows at the left side of the downstroke which turns to the right and forms the indirect arcs, and when the latter, which are unequal in size and dimension, may or may not have a loop in the center and may or may not join the initial downstroke,

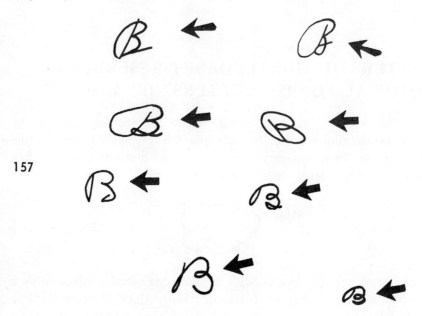

157

these are ANTIQUE LOCK PLATES and the writer pretends to be discreet but is very curious, indulges in gossip, and spreads rumors.

When in the printed B (3) after the downstroke is made the indirect arcs stand alone,

158

(this is the NUMBER 13)

or when the cursive b (6) begins with a slightly concave back of the loop followed by the downstroke below the loop and a final upcurve which ends in a loop, and when a final stroke, if any, turns in horizontal direction at the point where the crossing ends,

159

(these are the NUMBERS 6)

these are NUMBERS IN LETTERS and the writer craves money and possessions so intensely that he would do anything in his power to acquire them.

When in the cursive B (1), after the downstroke is made, the retrace stroke extends above it and curves into the upper indirect arc which is much greater in height than in width, and when the lower arc, which in turn is greater in height than in width and protrudes, retraces the upper arc to some extent and is almost parallel to it,

160   

these are GUIDING FINGERS and the writer is self-opinionated, convinced of his own wisdom and knows that his advice is the best that can be given.

When in the cursive B (1), after the downstroke is made, the retrace stroke extends above it and curves into the upper indirect arc followed by the lower indirect arc, and when the two arcs slant in different directions and form an angle in the center,

161

these are STUBBY FINGERS and the writer tries to gain his ends by harsh and rude measures.

When in the cursive B (1), after the downstroke is made, a straight retrace stroke or an upstroke extends high above the preceding downstroke and joins the upper indirect arc which is narrow, pointed, and much greater in height than in width, and when the lower arc, which in turn is greater in height than in width, protrudes and is almost parallel to the upper arc,

162

these are WARNING FINGERS and the writer seeks to gain the upper hand by intimidation and force.

When the cursive b (6) begins with the downstroke forming a narrow curve at the baseline, and when an upcurve follows which ends about halfway of the downstroke and has a tick-out stroke,

163

these are AUTHORITATIVE FINGERS and the writer has the tendency to browbeat and humiliate others.

When the cursive b (6) has a straight downstroke forming an angle with the upstroke which is almost straight and has a tick-out stroke,

164

these are POINTED FINGERS and the writer would not hesitate to coerce people into submission.

When in the cursive b (6) the crossing of the loop is low and the downstroke below the loop ends in a point or a narrow curve,

165

this is a CLUB and the writer is prone to enforce his will on others.

When in the cursive b (6) a straight downstroke, which ends in a point at the baseline, retraces the upstroke to some extent,

166

these are DAGGER BLADES and the writer, by using pressure and intimidation, tries to force people into his service.

When in the cursive b (6) the back of the loop and the downstroke below the loop are concave, and when the final upcurve curves back to the baseline and forms a loop,

167

this is a CONVENTIONAL EMBLEM and the writer pretends to be conservative and a stickler to principles in order to escape embarrassing situations.

When in the cursive b (6) the final upcurve touches the loop, and when the tick-out stroke is long and almost straight,

168

this is an UNUSABLE PROPELLER BLADE and the writer lacks force, drive, and initiative.

When in the cursive b (6) the final upcurve forms an angle with a long connecting stroke joining the succeeding cursive u (6), and when the space between the two letters widens towards the bottom,

169

this is a SACRIFICIAL BLOCK and the writer can be cruel and callous.

Chapter 16

LETTERS OF THE ALPHABET RESEMBLING
PICTORIAL FORMS: LETTERS "C" AND "c"

When the final upcurve of the Foreign C (4) curves back to the baseline and forms a loop,

170

this is a CONVENTIONAL EMBLEM and the writer pretends to be conservative and a stickler to principles in order to escape embarrassing situations.

When the cursive C (1) starts with a straight downstroke followed by a full curve, which may or may not retrace the preceding downstroke slightly, and ends in an almost straight horizontal stroke at the baseline,

171

this is a SICKLE and the writer is very discontented and has the urge to inflict injury.

When in the cursive C (1) the initial loop is incomplete, and when the downcurve, which is flat, ends abruptly at the baseline,

172

this is a BRACKET and the writer would not hesitate to use forceful means to control others.

When the cursive c (6) begins with a concave downcurve followed by a horizontal loop and the final downcurve,

173

this letter resembles the CURSIVE E (1) and the writer uses the ideas of others for his own benefit.

When the cursive c (6) starts at the baseline with a generously con-cave upstroke followed by a concave downstroke which joins the initial upstroke at the top and at the bottom,

174

this is a MOON ON THE WANE IN SMALL LETTERS and the writer at times is incompatible, uncooperative and contrary.

When the cursive c (6) slants to the left and the following cursive l (6) is vertical, and when the back of the loop is concave and the final stroke of the "l" swings to the right at the point where the crossing ends and joins the following cursive e (7) which slants to the right,

175

this is an UNUSABLE ANCHOR and the writer feels insecure, is irreso-lute, vacillating in his opinion, not steadfast in purpose, and will fre-quently change his course of action.

When the cursive c (6) begins with the downcurve followed by the connecting line joining the next cursive t (5) which has no bar, and when the downstroke of the latter, which ends abruptly at the baseline, retraces the preceding connecting line almost to the end,

176

or when in the cursive c (6) the straight initial upstroke forms an angle with a long tick, and when the full curve slightly retraces the tick and crosses the initial upstroke twice,

177

these are FISH HOOKS and the writer uses all kinds of tricks and ruses to get into the good graces of people planning to get something from them.

Chapter 17

LETTERS OF THE ALPHABET RESEMBLING
PICTORIAL FORMS: LETTERS "D" AND "d"

When the loop of the cursive D (1) extends beyond the left side of the downstroke and joins and/or crosses it,

178

these are LOOPS EXTENDING BEYOND THE LETTER and the writer cleverly hides malicious and perfidious designs.

When the printed D (3) is incomplete and ends in a concave stroke which extends below the line and ends in a curve turned up to the right,

179

this is an ALGA and the writer gives the impression of agreement and cooperation but seeks to accomplish his purpose by underhanded practice.

When in the printed D (3) after the downstroke is made, the half circle, which may touch the downstroke at the bottom or not at all, begins and ends at the left side of and is not at right angles with it,

180

these are OPEN EGG SHELLS and the writer who feels misunderstood, neglected, and underrated, compensates for his frustration by placing himself into the limelight.

When the cursive D (1) ends in a final upcurve, which does not join the initial downstroke, curves back to the baseline and ends before reaching it,

181

these are BROKEN EGG SHELLS and the writer can be easily hurt and takes such incidents so much to heart that he finds it difficult to forget them.

When in the printed D (3) the half circle stands alone and begins at the left side of and above the downstroke with a short, concave downcurve, and when a long horizontal stroke forms an angle with a long, convex, final downstroke which extends far below the baseline and ends in a point,

182

this is a SWAN and the writer uses all sorts of tricks and schemes to impress people and interest them for his plans.

When the downstroke of the printed D (3) is short and the half circle, which begins and ends at the left side of the downstroke, does not join the top and is greater in width than in height,

183

this is a MOUSE TRAP and the writer can find his way through the most devious roads because, being a trickster himself, he sees through the maneuverings of others.

When the initial downstroke of the cursive D (1) is straight and slants far to the right, and when the loop is parallel to slant of the downstroke, and when the short, final upcurve joins the initial downstroke at the top,

184

this is a CHESS PAWN ON ITS SIDE and the writer although he knows exactly what he wants, often pretends to be completely helpless. This is nothing but a pose to arouse people's sympathy.

When in the cursive D (1) the initial downstroke is long and straight, and when the loop or the triangle at the bottom is almost parallel to slant of the downstroke, and when the final upcurve ends in a loop crossing the downstroke twice,

185

these are HAND DRILLS and the writer can force others to accept his plans, ideas, and points of view.

When the printed D (3) begins at the baseline with an almost straight upstroke curving into a slightly convex downcurve which does not join the initial upstroke and ends below the baseline,

186

or when the downstroke of the printed D (3) is short, and when the half circle, which stands alone, begins above the downstroke and consists of a straight, upward slanting stroke curving into a long, straight downstroke which slants to the right and ends far below the baseline,

187

these are GIGANTIC WHIPS HELD UP and the writer can curb others' freedom of action by harsh and drastic measures.

When the half circle of the printed D (3) does not join the down-stroke and has a short curve at each end,

188

this is a BRACKET and the writer would not hesitate to use forceful means to control others.

When the cursive D (1) has a short, straight downstroke followed by a loop and a flat, much longer final upcurve, and when the latter which curves back to the baseline, touches the tip of the initial downstroke and ends on the preceding upcurve,

189

this is a FAULTY VIOLIN CLEF and the writer can cleverly speak of subject matters of which he has no previous knowledge.

When in the cursive D (2) or printed D (3), after the vertical down-stroke is made; the half circle, which begins and ends at the left side of the downstroke and does not join it, is parallel to slant of it,

190

this is a MAN IN THE MOON and the writer under the mask of guileless-ness, dignity, and kindness hides his selfish intentions.

When the cursive D (2) has a long, slightly concave downstroke ending in a point at the baseline, and when a short, slightly concave up-stroke partly retraces the preceding downstroke and forms an angle with a short, straight, left slanting downstroke which does not reach the base-line, and when a retrace stroke extends above the preceding downstroke and joins the tip of the initial downstroke,

190a

this is a CENSURING FINGER and the writer has the tendency to expose the imperfections of others and to reproach their shortcomings.

When the downstroke of the cursive D (2) or Foreign D (4, 5) begins with a left tending hook followed by a slightly concave downstroke and a wedge between the downstroke and the final upstroke, and when the final upcurve crosses the initial downstroke in the lower half,

191

or when the printed D (3) begins with a downstroke followed by a half circle , which is greater in width than in height, joins the tip of the downstroke, extends far beyond it to the left and ends in a left slanting hook, turned down,

192

or when the cursive D (2) or Foreign D (4, 5) begins with a slightly con-
.cave downstroke followed by a wedge between the downstroke and the final upstroke, which joins the downstroke at the top, extends above it, and ends in a hook turned down to the right,

193

these are HARPOONS and the writer is callous, cruel, and sadistic.

  When in the cursive D (1) the final upcurve is flat and ends in an e-loop followed by a final stroke which slants almost in the same direction as the preceding upcurve,

194

or when in the cursive d (7) the oval, which does not join the rest of the letter, begins with an almost horizontal stroke, and when an e-loop follows and a final stroke, which turns in horizontal direction at the point where the crossing ends, and slants almost in the same direction as the initial stroke,

195

these are STONES and the writer can make difficulties for others and put obstacles in their way so furtively that he cannot easily be held responsible.

When the upstroke of the cursive d (6) is decidedly convex and forms an angle with a long, straight, right tending, horizontal or upward slanting, final stroke,

196

these are PELICANS and the writer has the tendency to point out the weaknesses of others and by carping criticism undermines their self-confidence.

When the retrace downstroke of the cursive d (6) ends in or narrows to a point below the line,

197

this is a STING OF A WASP and the writer is given to bickering and provokes, criticizes, and belittles others.

When the oval of the cursive d (7) begins with a convex upcurve which is made within the oval, and when the rest of the letter does not reach the baseline,

198

this is a DREAMY EYE and the writer knows how to evoke the good will of others and to win their acceptance.

When the printed d (8) begins with a downstroke which does not reach the baseline, and when the incomplete oval slightly retraces the bottom of and is drawn around, below and beyond the downstroke,

199

these are AUTO GEAR SHIFTS and the writer is an autocratic person who insists on having his own will, seeks to curb and limit others, and does not easily allow them to speak their mind.

When the printed d (8) starts with the downstroke curving to the right at the baseline followed by a convex upcurve, which crosses the downstroke about halfway, curves back to and joins the downstroke almost at the baseline,

200

this is a PENDULUM and the writer is callous and ruthless in pursuing his aims.

When the cursive d (6) has a loop the back of which forms part of the preceding oval, and when the final stroke ends above the baseline,

201

these are UNUSABLE PROPELLER BLADES and the writer lacks force, drive, and initiative.

When the oval of the cursive d (7) starts with a long, almost straight, horizontal stroke above the baseline, and when the oval is drawn around the end of it followed by a vertical upstroke and a retrace stroke which do not reach the baseline,

202

this is an AUTOMATIC WARNING BELL OUT OF ORDER and the writer by plotting and scheming tries to checkmate people.

When the oval of the cursive d (6) is drawn around a short, left slanting downstroke and a short, right slanting upstroke forming an angle,

203

this is an EMBLEM OF A SECRET ALLIANCE and the writer assumes the appearance of loyalty and integrity to win the confidence of people and induce them to discard their reserve.

When the oval of the cursive d (6) is incomplete, followed by a loop which slants to the right and the crossing of which is low, and when the upstroke of the loop slants into the pointed top which is slightly retraced by the concave back of the loop,

204

this is a CANDLE WITH FLICKERING FLAME and the writer is apt to change his attitude towards his world unexpectedly and become disloyal.

When the oval of the cursive d (6) is incomplete, followed by a loop which slants in vertical direction and the crossing of which is low, and when the upstroke of the loop slants into the pointed top which is slightly retraced by the concave back of the loop,

205

this is a CANDLE WITH STEADY FLAME and the writer feigns warm feelings for others so that they believe him ready to sacrifice.

When in the cursive d (6, 7), after the oval is made, the upstroke has a double curve or is convex and ends in a short pointed loop, and when the downstroke below the loop is either straight, ends in a point and has a short final stroke or is convex and ends abruptly at the baseline,

206

these are SHEARS and the writer is cruel and his machinations are at times harmful.

When in the cursive d (6, 7), after the oval is made, an upstroke and a concave retrace stroke extending below the baseline, join the oval which is almost in the center of the succeeding strokes,

207

these are POT COVERS and the writer wants to have his way, under all circumstances enforce his will, and can become stubborn and unreasonable when his demands are resisted or denied.

When the cursive d (6) begins with an indirect oval at the baseline followed by a horizontal stroke ending in a direct loop, and when the connecting line joining the next cursive e (7) is almost horizontal and the downstroke below the loop turns in horizontal direction at the point where the crossing ends,

208

these are BUBBLES and the writer gives himself an air of importance by indulging in exaggeration.

When in the cursive d (6) the oval has a narrow curve at the bottom and the final down stroke does not reach the baseline,

209

this is a SPOON and the writer has the uncanny ability of finding people of whom he can take advantage.

When in the cursive d (6, 7), after the oval is made, the rest of the letter stands alone, and when the following cursive o (5) has no tick-out stroke and is almost parallel to the oval of the "d",

210

these are the FRACTIONS % and the writer is very calculating and figures everything in dollars and cents before he takes any action.

When in the cursive d (6) the oval is incomplete and slants to the left, and when the following upstroke slants to the left and then to the right forming a serpentine stroke which curves into the short, convex, left slanting downstroke of the succeeding cursive s (8),

211

this is a GROVELLING SNAKE and the writer can be friendly towards a person one day and betray him the next.

When in the cursive d (6) the upstroke following the oval is short and the retrace stroke does not reach the baseline, and when a long connecting line curves into the convex downstroke of the following cursive s (8) which ends in a point at the baseline,

212

this is a DOUBLE HOOK and the writer grasps every opportunity to succeed even at the expense of others.

Chapter 18

LETTERS OF THE ALPHABET RESEMBLING PICTORIAL FORMS: LETTERS "E" AND "e"

When in the cursive E (1) the upper part begins with a direct horizontal loop, if any, and when the center loop is substituted by a convex curve followed by the lower direct arc ending at the baseline,

213   ℰ   ℰ   ℰ   Ɛ   ℰ

these are GLITTERING SNAKES and the writer can be so affable, kind, and obliging that others trust him and do not believe him capable of wriggling out of situations which burden him with too much responsibility.

When the cursive E (2) begins with an undercurved upstroke ending in a left slanting loop, and when the center part is substituted by a protruding convex curve followed by a decidedly concave lower direct arc,

214   ℛ

these are BODIES WITH CHEST OUT, HEAD BACK and the writer feigns dependence, a clever maneuver to exert influence over others.

When the cursive E (2) begins with a short upstroke ending in a loop, and when the center part is substituted by a slightly convex curve followed by a slightly concave, lower direct arc, and when the final stroke is almost straight,

215   ℰ

this is a GRACEFUL BODY and the writer is charming and gives the impression of being very agreeable.

When the Foreign E (6) is vertical and the center part is substituted by a slightly convex curve followed by the lower direct arc ending in a long, straight, horizontal, final stroke,

216   ℰ

this is a BODY WITH OUTSTRETCHED LEGS and the writer has the ability to impress his world by poise and self-control.

When the cursive E (2) starts with an oblong horizontal, deflated, direct loop followed by an identical center loop and the lower direct arc,

217   → Ɛ

these are GRASPING FINGERS and the writer very quickly takes advantage of any and every opportunity which will benefit him.

When the center bar of the printed E (3) is in the lower part of the downstroke,

218   E ←

these are TWO ROOMS, A SMALLER AND A LARGER, and the writer is not easily friendly and conceals his true self under a mask of conventionality.

When the top bar of the printed E (3) is above the downstroke,

219   E ←

this is a ROOM WITH OPEN CEILING and the writer has the desire to plunge into an unconventional life.

When two bars of the printed E (3) which have the same length, do not join the downstroke,

220   E ←

this is a ROOM WITH PARTITION WALLS and the writer is not very thorough in his work and inclined to overlook important details.

When in the printed E (3, 4) one or more bars, which may be curved or straight, end in a point or hook, and when they either form an angle or a curve with the downstroke at the top and/or at the bottom,

221   Ɛ   Ɛ   Ɛ

these are BELT BUCKLES and the writer is callous and ruthless in pursuing his aims.

When the cursive E (2) begins with a long, straight upstroke at the baseline followed by a very short, straight, left slanting downstroke which forms an angle with the upper direct arc, and when the two arcs, which are connected by a convex center curve, cross the initial upstroke four times, and when the letter does not reach the baseline,

222

this is a MEDICAL SYMBOL and the writer under the mask of readiness and willingness to help camouflages his malicious intentions.

When the upper direct arc of the cursive E (2) consists of a generous curve followed by a convex center curve, and when the lower direct arc consists of a straight downstroke which ends in a point,

223

this is a LARGE HOOK and the writer takes advantage of others by re-sorting to bluff and trickery.

When in the cursive E (1) a long, straight upstroke starts far below the baseline, curves to the left at the top and back to the baseline forming a long, narrow loop, followed by a circular center loop, and when the lower direct arc crosses the initial upstroke and ends in a large loop,

224

this is a HAND DRILL and the writer can force others to accept his plans, ideas, and points of view.

When the upper direct arc of the cursive E (2) consists of a con-cave, left slanting downcurve followed by a large protruding loop and a final stroke,

225

or when in the cursive e (7), after the upstroke and the loop are made, the final upstroke turns to the right at the point where the crossing ends and slants almost in the same direction as the initial upstroke,

226

these are STONES and the writer can make difficulties for others and put obstacles in their way so furtively that he cannot easily be held responsible.

When in the cursive E (2) the direct arcs are greater in width than in height, the center part is decidedly convex or pointed, and the final stroke is long, straight, and slants downwards or in horizontal direction,

227

these are PROVOCATIVE BODIES and the writer applies his captivating and alluring charm to convey the impression of being ready to yield to the wishes and desires of others but can reverse his attitude unexpectedly and wriggle out of a situation.

When in the successive cursive "ei," "en" (7, 6), "er" (7) the last letter consists of a serpentine stroke ending below the baseline,

228

these are SQUIRMING BODIES and the writer yields to his strong desires and appetites.

When the cursive e (7) begins with a short initial upstroke followed by a loop, which is greater in width than in height, and when the downstroke below the loop is eliminated and the horizontal final stroke is longer than and not at level with the initial upstroke,

229

this is an INFANT WITH FLATTENED HEAD and the writer can become headstrong and obstinate.

When the cursive e (7) begins with an upward slanting or horizontal stroke followed by a loop which is out of proportion, and when the downstroke below the loop is eliminated or almost eliminated and the final stroke either is shorter or longer than and not at level with the initial stroke,

230

this is an INFANT and the writer pretends helplessness to arouse the sympathy of others and assure their aid.

When the cursive e (7) begins with a concave downstroke above the baseline followed by a concave horizontal stroke and the "e-loop," and when the downstroke below the loop is eliminated or almost eliminated and the concave, horizontal, final stroke is similar in form and size to the initial strokes,

231

these are SPIDERS and the writer is very smart in handling people, can win them by charm and affability, and like a spider, can get them into his web.

Chapter 19

LETTERS OF THE ALPHABET RESEMBLING PICTORIAL FORMS: LETTERS "F" AND "f"

When in the cursive F (1a) at the lowest tip of the downstroke a left tending indirect loop follows,

232

this is a LEFT TENDING ADDITIONAL LOOP and the writer cleverly hides malicious and perfidious designs.

When the cursive F (2) starts with a short, convex, horizontal stroke curving into a short, convex downstroke which ends in a point at the baseline, and when the bar is convex and has almost the same length as the preceding stroke,

233

this is a CRAB and the writer's machinations are at times shady and harmful.

When the upper bar of the printed F (4) is above the downstroke, and when the center bar, which crosses the downstroke, is approximately twice as long on the right side,

234

this is a FALLEN CROSS and the writer pretends to cherish ideals and to muster all his power for them.

When the downstroke of the printed F (3, 4) slopes to the left and the upper bar is made above it, and when the center bar crosses it in the upper half and is almost at right angles to it,

235

this is a TOTTERING CROSS and the writer shows little respect for others, their actions, and achievements.

When the cursive F (2) or Foreign F (5) begins with a concave, right tending upstroke curving into the downstroke which ends in a point at the baseline,

236

these are SHEPHERD'S CROOKS and the writer is inclined to mix into the affairs of others.

When in the printed F (3, 4), after the downstroke is made, the top bar, which begins at the left side and is longer at the right of the downstroke, is convex, slants down, and narrows to a point,

237   F

this is a SHOEMAKER'S HAMMER and the writer enjoys making people feel small.

When the cursive F (2) begins with a straight, long, left tending downstroke which forms an angle with a slightly concave, right tending upstroke, and when the upstroke in turn forms an angle with a straight, final downstroke ending in a point at the baseline,

238

this is a SCYTHE and the writer is ruthless and unscrupulous.

When the cursive F (2), which has a long center bar, starts with a concave, almost horizontal curve forming an angle with a straight downstroke, which in turn forms an angle with a left tending, convex, horizontal curve at the baseline,

239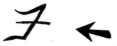

this is a DEVIL'S FORK and the writer under the mask of kindness and service, can cause all kinds of difficulties and confusion.

When the upper bar of the printed F (3, 4), which is long and straight, is above the downstroke and ends in a hook or curve turned down to the left,

240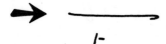

this is a RIDING CROP HELD TO THE RIGHT and the writer has the tendency to control people and situations by forcible means.

When the cursive F (2) has a short initial downstroke and the bar, if any, does not join or cross it, and when the horizontal final curve extends to the left and curves into a long, straight or almost straight, right tending, horizontal stroke above the downstroke,

241

or when in the cursive F (1), at the lowest point of the straight downstroke, a left tending, convex, upward slanting stroke follows, which decidedly curves to the left at the end and joins the cap, which consists of a straight stroke only,

242

these are TRAINERS' WHIPS and the writer strives to control situations by pestering, harassing and vexing people so that they are unable to offer resistance.

When the cursive F (2) starts below the baseline with a long, concave upstroke curving into the straight downstroke ending in a point at the baseline,

243

this is a WHIP WITH LONG LASH and the writer by restricting people in their freedom of action and depriving them of their peace of mind, seeks to have mastery over them.

When in the cursive f (7) the upstroke of the lower loop crosses the downstroke at the baseline and forms a second loop at the left side of the downstroke,

244

this is a LEFT TENDING ADDITIONAL LOOP ON THE LINE and the writer finds it difficult to forget a wrong.

When in the cursive f (7) the upstroke of the lower loop crosses the downstroke before it reaches the baseline and forms an angle with a straight, right tending, final stroke which in turn crosses the downstroke,

245

these are NOMADIC TENTS and the writer is extremely restless, unstable and fickle.

When the upper part of the cursive f (7) is almost eliminated, the lower loop is long and forms a narrow curve at the bottom, and when the upstroke of the loop crosses the downstroke almost at the top,

246

these are LONG FISHES and the writer is callous and cruel.

When in the cursive f (7), at the lowest tip, and at the left side of the downstroke, an upstroke follows which is close to the downstroke and ends in a left tending, indirect loop,

247

these are RETROGRADE STROKES and ADDITIONAL LEFT TENDING LOOPS ON THE LINE and the writer cannot forget a wrong and will seek revenge at a time when people do not in the least expect it and do not suspect him as the originator of their troubles.

When in the cursive f (7), at the lowest point of the downstroke, a left tending, straight upstroke follows, which forms an angle with or slightly retraces the downstroke, and when a right tending, concave, final stroke, which crosses the downstroke, forms an angle with or slightly retraces the preceding upstroke,

248

these are PLIERS BELOW THE LINE and the writer would not hesitate using any means serving his ends.

When in the cursive f (7), at the lowest point of the downstroke, a left tending, convex, upward slanting curve retraces the downstroke to some extent, and when a straight, right tending, upward slanting, final stroke retraces the end of the preceding curve and crosses the downstroke,

249

these are WEBBED FEET and the writer can hide his selfish intentions so cleverly that people who later notice that they have been taken advantage of, are quite surprised that he is capable of such an act.

When in the Foreign f (8) the downstroke below the line narrows to a point,

250

this is a STING OF A WASP and the writer is given to bickering and provokes, criticizes, and belittles others.

When in the Foreign f (8) the upper loop is bent forward more than the part below the line,

251

this is a BODY WITH HEAD BENT FORWARD and the writer by subservience and apparent devotion gives the impression of completely agreeing with the ideas and wishes of others in order better to achieve his aims.

When the cursive f (7) is loopless and pointed at the top, and when the downstroke is shorter above the line, straight or slightly concave, and ends in a point below the line, and when a straight or curved upstroke slightly retraces or forms a narrow curve with the preceding downstroke, and when a decidedly concave final stroke retraces the end of the upstroke,

252

these are CENSURING FINGERS and the writer has the tendency to expose the imperfection of others and to reproach their shortcomings.

When the long upstroke of the cursive f (7) is partly retraced by a long, decidedly concave downstroke ending below the line,

253

this is the EIFFEL TOWER and there are no limits to this writer's striving for power and his desire to gain the ascendency.

When in the cursive f (7) the crossing of the upper loop is low, and when the initial upstroke and the upstroke of the lower loop, which has a horizontal final stroke, join, and when the part below has almost the same length as the part above the line,

254

these are UNUSABLE PROPELLER BLADES and the writer lacks force, drive, and initiative.

When in the cursive f (7) the lower loop is pointed and has an upstroke ending in a small loop which joins the downstroke at the baseline,

255

these are QUIVERS and the writer is bitterly vindictive.

When the cursive f (7) begins with a short, convex upcurve or a horizontal curve to the left followed by the downstroke above and below the line, and when the upstroke of the lower loop is at the left side of the downstroke,

256

or when in the cursive f (7), after the part above the line is made, the downstroke below the line ends in a short, concave, left tending curve,

257

these are DENTAL INSTRUMENTS FOR DIAGNOSIS and the writer is extremely clever at sounding people out, observing the imperfection of them and using the information to his own advantage.

When the cursive f (7) has no upper loop, and when the upstroke of the lower loop, which is at the left side and at least half the length of the downstroke, may or may not join it,

258

or when the cursive f (7) has no upper loop and the upstroke of the lower loop, which is at least half the length of the letter, crosses the downstroke,

259

or when in the cursive f (7), which may or may not have an upper loop, the upstroke of the lower loop, which is incomplete, ends in a point and is at least half the length of the letter,

260

these are WHIPS HELD DOWN and the writer has the tendency to subjugate and tyrannize people.

When the cursive f (7) starts with a hook or curve turned up followed by a long initial upstroke which curves into the long downstroke ending in a point below the line,

261

or when the cursive f (7) begins with a short, left slanting hook, which is slightly retraced by a long, decidedly concave upstroke curving into a long downstroke, which ends in a point below the line,

262

these are GIGANTIC WHIPS HELD UP and the writer can curb others' freedom of action by harsh and drastic measures.

When the cursive f (7) has a short initial upstroke high above the baseline followed by a short upper loop and the downstroke ending in a point below the line,

263

these are WHIPS HELD UP and the writer exercises authority to have mastery of people and situations.

When in the cursive f (7) the loops are pointed and similar in form and size, and when the upstroke of the lower loop is concave and at the left side of the downstroke, and when the initial upstroke slants almost in the same direction as the final,

264

these are FAN BLADES and the writer can adapt himself to others so adroitly that they think he is highly interested in them and take his words at face value, while in reality he has mental reservations.

When in the cursive f (7) the upper and the lower loops are different in form and size, and when the upstroke of the lower loop is concave and at the left side of the downstroke, and when the initial upstroke slants almost in the same direction as the final,

265

these letters resemble the GERMAN SCRIPT h (9) and the writer is skilled at duping and tricking people.

When in the cursive f (7), after the part above the line is made, the downstroke below the line forms an angle with the upstroke of the lower loop, and when the latter is at the left side of the downstroke, widens at the end, turns to the right, crosses the downstroke, and ends in a slightly upward slanting direction,

266

these are POWERFUL SCISSORS and if the writer should not get results by trickery, he will resort to force.

When in the cursive f (7), at the end of the convex downstroke a left tending, concave, horizontal curve and a retrace stroke follow curving into a convex final upstroke which joins the downstroke,

267

this is a COMET and the writer associates only with those from whom he hopes to gain and withdraws from those which burden him with responsibility.

When in the cursive f (7), which may or may not have an upper loop, the final downstroke ending in a point is at least as long or longer above than below the line, and when it is slightly retraced by the upstroke of the lower loop which is close to the preceding downstroke,

268

these are KNIVES and the writer is embittered and hateful.

When the cursive f (7) begins with the final downstroke followed by the lower loop which is narrow at the bottom and widens at the center, and when its upstroke crosses the downstroke at least halfway and ends shortly beyond it,

269

these are UNUSABLE SABERS and the writer has malicious joy in playing tricks on others.

When the downstroke of the Foreign printed f (9) is long and has a double curve ending in a short curve turned up to the left, and when the bar is in the upper half of the downstroke,

270

f

this is a TURKISH SWORD and the writer is cruel and has sadistic tendencies.

Chapter 20

LETTERS OF THE ALPHABET RESEMBLING PICTORIAL FORMS: LETTERS "G" AND "g"

When in the cursive G (1) the downstroke ends in a point followed by a convex, left tending curve,

271

these are REVERSED STROKES and the writer while enjoying the reputation as a man of fine character, would not hesitate to slander a person.

When the initial upstroke of the cursive G (1) is partly retraced and forms a narrow, concave, horizontal center curve with the following upstroke, which is almost as long as, and parallel to the preceding retrace (down) stroke, and is retraced by the final downstroke,

272

these are GRASPING FINGERS and the writer very quickly takes advantage of any and every opportunity which will benefit him.

When the printed G (3) is greater in height than in width, and when the final upcurve slants to the left followed by a horizontal final stroke which extends to the right and beyond the letter,

273

this is an AUTO GEAR SHIFT and the writer is an autocratic person who insists on having his own will, seeks to curb and limit others, and does not easily allow them to speak their mind.

When in the cursive G (2) the incomplete oval is greater in width than in height, and when a straight downstroke forms an angle with the preceding oval at the baseline and ends in a point below the line,

274

this is a SICKLE and the writer is very discontented and has the urge to inflict injury.

When in the Foreign G (5) the final downstroke ends in a point, and when the long, initial upstroke of any following letter crosses it,

275

this is a DIAGONAL CROSSING and the writer can create strife and confusion and seriously interfere with the plans of others.

When in the Foreign G (5) the downstroke below the upper loop extends below the baseline and ends in a point, and when a final upstroke follows, which is at the right side of the downstroke, retraces it to some extent, and joins the succeeding cursive e (7), and when either the final downstroke or the upstroke is curved,

276

or when in the cursive g (7), after the part above the line is made, the downstroke below the line ends in a point, and when the final upstroke, which is at the right side of the downstroke and retraces it to some extent, joins the following cursive e (7), which may be higher or lower than the preceding letter, and when either the final downstroke or the upstroke is curved,

277

these are BELLOWS and the writer is a show off and to reach his objective resorts to all sorts of tricks and ruses.

When in the Foreign G (6a) the downstroke below the line consists of a concave curve only,

278

or when in the Foreign G (6) the downstroke below the line has a double
curve ending in a concave curve turned up to the left,

279

or when in the cursive g (7) the downstroke below the line ends either in
a point followed by a short hook turned up, or in a short curve turned up,
or when the downstroke is concave and ends in a point,

280

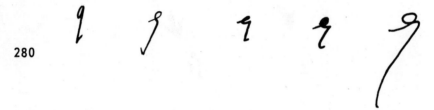

these are ALGAE and the writer gives the impression of agreement and
cooperation but seeks to accomplish his purpose by underhanded practice.

When the cursive G (1) has an additional loop, which is different in
form and size, at the top of the downstroke,

281

or when in the cursive G (1), after the initial upstroke and the loop are
made, a straight or slightly concave upstroke follows which slants almost
in the same direction as the initial upstroke,

282

or when in the cursive g (7) the part above the line consists of an undercurved, initial upstroke ending in a loop and followed by an upward slanting stroke, which turns to the right at the point where the crossing ends,
and slants almost in the same direction as the initial upstroke,

283

these are STONES and the writer can make difficulties for others and put
obstacles in their way so furtively that he cannot easily be held responsible.

    When the printed G (3) has a decidedly concave downstroke, and
when the final upcurve ends in a loop,

284

or when in the cursive g (7) the oval is incomplete and the upcurve ends
in a loop,

285

these are the NUMBERS 6 and the writer craves money and possessions
so intensely that he would do anything in his power to acquire them.

    When in the cursive g (7, 8) the downstroke below the line ends in a
point and is slightly retraced by a left tending, convex, upward slanting
stroke, and when a straight, right tending, final upstroke follows which
slightly retraces the preceding upstroke and may or may not join the downstroke,

286

these are WEBBED FEET and the writer hides his selfish intentions so
cleverly that people who later notice that they have been taken advantage
of are quite surprised that he is capable of such an act.

    When in the cursive g (7, 8) the upstroke of the lower loop swings
to the left and forms an indirect horizontal loop with a straight, right
tending stroke which crosses the downstroke,

287

this is a LEFT TENDING ADDITIONAL LOOP BELOW THE LINE and the writer can be vengefully malevolent.

When the cursive g (7) begins with a short, convex, left tending, horizontal upcurve followed by a short, horizontal stroke curving into the downstroke, which has a double curve,

288

this is a VENOMOUS SNAKE and the writer through charm, affability, and diplomacy can win the acceptance and confidence of people so that they do not recognize his false nature.

When in the cursive g (7, 8) the final downstroke ends in a point, and when the following upstroke of the lower loop which is shaped like one-half of an ellipse, is decidedly concave, and ends on the downstroke or crosses it, and has a very short final stroke,

289

this is a MOON ON THE WANE IN LOWER LOOPS and the writer is changeable in his moods and in his attitude towards and sympathies for people.

When in the printed g (9) the downstroke below the line narrows to a point,

290

this is a STING OF A WASP and the writer is given to bickering and provokes, criticizes, and belittles people.

When the cursive g (7) begins with a short, initial upstroke followed by a loop and a short, concave, left slanting downstroke, and when the latter curves into the downstroke below the line which has a double curve,

291

this is a SENSUOUS BODY and the writer can fascinate and allure others and make them virtually slaves.

When in the cursive g (7) the oval is incomplete, and when the downstroke below the line is straight and ends in a point, and when the final upstroke, which may be straight or slightly curved, slightly retraces the downstroke, is at the right side of it, and ends in a point below the line,

292

these are CENSURING FINGERS and the writer has the tendency to expose the imperfection of others and to reproach their shortcomings.

When in the cursive g (7, 8) the oval is incomplete and begins with a short, convex upcurve or with a short horizontal curve followed by the downcurve which extends into the part below the line,

293

these are DENTAL INSTRUMENTS FOR DIAGNOSIS and the writer is extremely clever at sounding people out, observing the imperfection of them and using the information to his own advantage.

When in the cursive g (7, 8) the part above the line consists of a deflated oval or a small, ink-filled loop or a period followed by the rest of the letter,

294

or when in the cursive g (8) the incomplete oval consists of a flat down-curve followed by an almost horizontal stroke which curves into the part below the line,

295

these are DENTAL INSTRUMENTS FOR FILLING CAVITIES and the writer would not hesitate to use force and even pressure to make others pliable to his wishes.

When in the cursive g (7) the oval is incomplete and the final down-stroke retraces the shorter upcurve, and when the upstroke of the lower loop, which is incomplete, ends in a point shortly below the baseline,

296

this is a WHIP HELD DOWN and the writer has the tendency to subjugate and tyrannize people.

When the oval of the cursive g (7, 8) is open at the top,

297

these letters resemble the CURSIVE "y" and the writer has little power of resistance to temptation and may act irresponsible.

When the incomplete oval of the cursive g (7) consists of a concave downcurve followed by an e-loop on top of the final downstroke extending into the part below the line,

298

this letter resembles the GERMAN SCRIPT H (10) and the writer is skilled at duping and tricking people.

When in the cursive g (7) the downstroke below the line forms an angle with a left tending, straight, upward slanting stroke which in turn forms an angle with a right tending, final upstroke,

299

this is a TRIANGLE BELOW THE LINE and the writer uses underhanded and cruel means to weaken and control others.

When in the cursive g (7, 8) the downstroke below the line is decidedly convex and forms an angle with a straight, final upstroke,

300

or when the cursive g (7, 8) slants decidedly to the right and at the lowest point of the final downstroke curves to the left followed by an almost horizontal stroke which forms an angle with a straight final upstroke ending on the preceding downstroke,

301

these are SINKING ROW BOATS and the writer when his patience dwindles and his zeal cools, will turn his back on all his responsibility.

When in the cursive g (7), after the oval is made, the downstroke below the line forms an angle with a left tending upstroke which widens at the end, curves abruptly to the right, and ends before it reaches the baseline,

302

these are SAIL BOATS and the writer is fickle, apt to change his course of action as well as his sympathies for people unexpectedly.

When in the consecutive cursive "gh," "gl," "ga" (7, 6), "gr" (7) one of the letters is higher than the other,

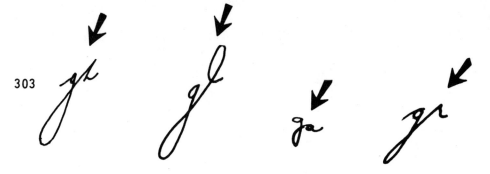

303

and/or when in the consecutive cursive "ge" (7), "go" (7, 5) the loops are inflated,

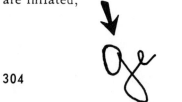

304

and/or when the connecting line between the consecutive cursive "go" (7, 5) or "ga" (7, 6) is extremely long,

305

and/or when in the cursive "ge" (7) the upstroke of the lower loop crosses the downstroke before it reaches the baseline,

306

these are UNUSABLE SURGICAL INSTRUMENTS and the writer is shrewd and crafty and uses all sorts of tricks and schemes to gain his end.

When in the cursive g (7, 8), after the part above the line is made, the downstroke below the line ends in a point, and when the upstroke of the lower loop widens at the end, turns to the right before it reaches the baseline, crosses the downstroke and curves into the following cursive "e", and when one of the letters is higher than the other,

307

these are LARGE SHEARS and the writer is callous and ruthless in pursuing his aims.

Chapter 21

LETTERS OF THE ALPHABET RESEMBLING PICTORIAL FORMS: LETTERS "H" AND "h"

When in the cursive H (1) the center loop, which is large and may or may not be completed, extends beyond the left side of the initial downstroke,

308

these are LOOPS EXTENDING BEYOND THE LETTER and the writer cleverly hides malicious and perfidious designs.

When the printed H (3) and the cursive H (1), which has a straight final downstroke and a deflated loop in the center, begin with a generously convex downstroke,

309

these are HORNS and the writer can become very obstinate and stubborn and will insist upon carrying out his ideas regardless of opposition and consequences.

When the initial stroke of the printed H (3), which begins at the baseline, has a long retrace stroke followed by a concave, horizontal, center curve, and when the upstroke of the curve is retraced by the final downstroke,

310

these are GRASPING FINGERS and the writer very quickly takes advantage of any and every opportunity which will benefit him.

When in the cursive H (1), at the lowest tip of the first downstroke, a long, undercurved upstroke follows, which forms angles with the preceding and the following downstroke, and when the second downstroke is straight, longer than the first one, and ends in a point,

311

this is a GIGANTIC TOWER and the writer is apt to lose patience and interest in things or matters and give them up unexpectedly.

When in the printed H (3) one of the downstrokes is shorter than the other and the downstrokes are uneven either at the bottom or at the top or at the two,

312

or when the bar of the printed H (3) does not join the two downstrokes,

313

these are UNSAFE LADDERS and the writer can trick, trap, and outwit people.

When in the printed H (3) the downstrokes are not parallel and the distance between them is wider at the bottom than at the top,

314

this letter resembles the PRINTED "A" and the writer is irresolute and vacillating.

When the initial stroke of the Foreign H (5) is straight and slants upwards, and when the second part of the letter is higher than the first one, ends in a point above the baseline and has a final stroke which is identical to the initial stroke,

315

this is a HERALDIC SYMBOL and the writer tries to impress his world as trustworthy and reliable by pretending to be punctillious about conventions.

When the second part of the printed H (3) stands alone, and when the second downstroke is short, and the bar which crosses the downstroke in the center, is much longer on the left side,

316

this is a FALLEN CROSS and the writer pretends to cherish ideals and to muster all his power for them.

When the second downstroke of the cursive H (1) is straight and ends in a point above the baseline followed by a left tending and a right tending concave curve,

317

this is a MINER'S PICK and the writer resorts to force and pressure to attain his goal.

When in the printed H (3), after the downstrokes are made, the bar crosses them in the center and is much longer on the right side,

318

this is a GLASS CUTTER and the writer agrees with the adage that the end justifies the means.

When in the cursive H (2), at the lowest tip of a long, first down-stroke, a short, straight, left tending, and upward slanting stroke forms an angle with the concave, right tending, center stroke which crosses the first downstroke,

319

or when the second part of the cursive H (2) stands alone, and when at the lowest tip of a long, second downstroke, a short, straight, left tend-ing, upward slanting stroke forms an angle with the long, concave, right tending, final stroke which crosses the downstroke,

320

these are PLIERS and the writer tries to attain his aims by forcible means.

When in the cursive H (2) the first downstroke ends in a small curve turned up,

321

this is a RIDING CROP HELD DOWN and the writer seeks to control a situation by forcing his will on others so inconspicuously that they are not aware of his dictatorial intentions.

When in the cursive H (2) the second part stands alone, and when the second downstroke forms an angle with a short straight or slightly concave, left tending upstroke curving into a short straight, right tending, horizontal, final stroke which crosses the downstroke about one-third above the baseline,

322

these are SABERS LIFTED and the writer has the tendency to provoke others by resorting to a downright aggressive and offensive attitude.

When in the cursive H (2) the second part stands alone, and when the second downstroke forms an angle with a short, straight or slightly concave, left tending upstroke curving into a short, straight, right tending horizontal connecting line, and when the latter crosses the second down-stroke about one-third above the baseline and joins the following cursive o (5) which does not reach the baseline,

323

these are SABERS FASTENED and the writer weakens in his endeavors to fight for a cause and in spite of the best of intentions, he can be induced to alter his course.

When the bar of the printed H (3) starts with a short, concave curve, turned up or down, and crosses both downstrokes,

324

these are RIDING CROPS ON TWO STEMS and the writer's domineering tendencies are so powerful that he can seriously interfere with the plans of others.

When in the printed H (3) one or both downstrokes end with short hooks or curves turned up, and when the bar, which crosses both downstrokes, ends with a hook or curved turned up or down,

325

these are RIDING CROPS ONE UPON THE OTHER and the writer enjoys harassing and tormenting others and showing them that he has them in his power.

When in the printed H (3) the second part stands alone, and when the bar crosses the second downstroke in the middle and joins the tip of the following cursive i (6) which has a straight downstroke ending in a point above the baseline,

326

this is the NUMBER 4 and the writer craves money and possessions so intensely that he would do anything in his power to acquire them.

When in the printed H (3) the downstrokes, which may have the same length or the second one may be shorter than the first one, are convex and connected by a short bar,

327

these are AIRPLANES CIRCLING TO THE LEFT and the writer is inclined to evade situations which entail too much responsibility.

When in the printed H (3) the downstrokes, which may have the same length or the second one may be longer than the first one, are concave and connected by a short bar,

328

these are AIRPLANES CIRCLING TO THE RIGHT and the writer has the tendency to sound people out and gain information which will be of advantage to him.

When in the cursive H (2), after the initial downstroke is made, the second downstroke does not reach the baseline and ends in a left tending, concave, horizontal curve crossing the preceding downstroke, and when a straight or concave, right tending, horizontal final stroke ends on or crosses the second downstroke,

329

these are ROW BOATS and the writer dislikes committing himself and will cleverly extricate himself from situations which burden him with too much responsibility.

When the first downstroke of the cursive H (2), which is separated from the second one, consists of a double curve,

330

or when the downstroke of the printed h (7) begins with a short hook or curve and may be round at the baseline, and when the hump is partly round followed by the final downstroke which slants to the left,

331

these are DEMONIAC PROFILES OF NOSES and the writer enjoys creating confusion and dissension using schemes and plots so cunningly that no one holds him responsible.

When the cursive h (6) is loopless, the downstroke is pointed at the top and round at the baseline followed by a generously convex curve which widens towards the bottom and ends below the baseline,

332

this is a PROFILE OF NOSE WITH WIDE NOSTRIL and the writer has malicious joy in surreptitiously inflicting injury.

When the cursive h (6) is loopless, the downstroke is pointed at the top, convex and may be round at the baseline, and when the hump is partly round followed by the final downstroke, which slants to the left and ends below the baseline, and by the final upstroke,

333

these are PROFILES OF PUG NOSES and the writer is prone to vex and humiliate others by sarcastic and cynical remarks.

When the cursive h (6) is loopless and the downstroke is pointed at the top, and when the hump is partly round followed by the final downstroke, which slants to the left and ends below the baseline, and the final upstroke,

334

this is a PROFILE OF POINTED NOSE and the writer is sarcastic and cynical and does not admit a single good quality in others.

When the cursive h (6) is loopless, the initial downstroke is pointed at the top, decidedly concave, and may be partly round at the bottom, and when the second part of the letter, which may be partly round or pointed at the top and does not retrace the preceding downstroke, has a left slanting, final downstroke ending on or below the baseline and may or may not have a final upstroke,

335

these are PROFILES OF HOOKED NOSES and the writer can be friendly to one's face but at the same time harbor malicious and wicked designs.

When the cursive h (6) is loopless and the initial downstroke, which slants in vertical direction or to the left, is pointed at the top and partly round at the bottom, and when the second part of the letter, which may be partly round or pointed at the top, has a left slanting final downstroke ending above or on the baseline and may or may not have a final upstroke,

336

these are PROFILES OF NOSES WITH BOWED HEAD and the writer at times is so ill-humored that he vents his spleen on others.

When in the cursive h (6), after the initial downstroke and the retrace stroke are made, the final downstroke slants to the left, does not reach the baseline and may have a final stroke,

337

these are SHARP BEAKS and the writer seeks to provoke others by pointing out their shortcomings and reproaching them for them.

When the cursive h (6) is loopless, the initial downstroke is pointed at the top and ends in a deflated loop which is parallel to slant and at the left side of it, and when the second part of the letter has a left slanting, final downstroke ending above the baseline,

338

this is a DULL BEAK and the writer is callous and ruthless in pursuing his aims.

When in the cursive h (6) the crossing of the loop is low and the downstroke below the loop, which ends in a curve, is short, and when the final downstroke, which is not parallel to slant of the preceding down-stroke, may be pointed at the top and end on or below the baseline,

339

these are CHAMAELEONS and the writer is a turncoat, prone to shift his ground, not to stick to his colors or to adhere to his opinion.

When in the cursive h (6), which may be loopless, the downstroke forms a narrow curve at the baseline with the following upstroke and the hump which may be partly round or pointed, and when the concave, final downstroke which slants to the left or retraces the preceding upstroke, does not reach the baseline and has a final upstroke,

340

these are AUTHORITATIVE FINGERS and the writer has the tendency to browbeat and humiliate others.

When in the cursive h (6) the crossing of the loop is low and the downstroke below the loop is close to the initial upstroke,

341

these are CLUBS and the writer enforces his will on others.

When the cursive h (6) is loopless, pointed at the top, and when the hump is pointed and the final downstroke is concave, does not reach the baseline, and has a final upstroke,

342

these are INDEX FINGERS and the writer can present, demonstrate, and explain things very convincingly.

When in the cursive h (6) the initial upstroke forms an angle with the left slanting downstroke, and when the space between the upstroke and the downstroke is at least as wide or wider than the height of the strokes, and when the final downstroke ends in a point below the baseline,

343

this is a TENT and the writer is looking for thrills and sensations to overcome his feelings of loneliness, restlessness, and frustration.

When in the printed h (7, 8), after the downstroke is made, the following hump consists of a straight horizontal stroke forming an angle with the final downstroke which ends above or below the baseline,

344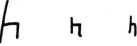

these are CHAIRS WITH BROKEN LEGS and the writer can trick, trap, and outwit people.

When in the printed h (7, 8), after the downstroke is made, the following hump consists of a straight, upward slanting stroke forming an angle with the final downstroke which ends above the baseline,

345

this is a CHAIR WITH SLANTED SEAT and the writer can trick, trap, and outwit people.

When in the printed h (7, 8), after the straight or convex, initial downstroke, the retrace stroke and the hump are made, the final downstroke has a double curve or is convex,

346

or when in the cursive h (6) the downstroke retraces the initial upstroke almost to the end, and when the second part of the letter consists of a retrace stroke followed by a straight, left slanting downstroke ending in a point at the baseline,

347

these are DEVIL'S FORKS and the writer under the mask of kindness and service, can cause all kinds of difficulties and confusion.

When in the cursive h (6) the upstroke of the inflated loop begins at the right side of the downstroke and does not join it,

348

this is a WHIP HELD UP and the writer exercises authority to have mastery of people and situations.

When the downstroke of the cursive h (6) retraces the initial upstroke to some extent, and when the second part of the letter, which is pointed at the top, is not parallel to slant of the preceding downstroke and does not reach the baseline,

349

these are DAGGER BLADES and the writer by using pressure and intimidation seeks to force people into his services.

When the second part of the cursive h (6) has a concave final downstroke which is pointed at the top and does not reach the baseline, and when a horizontal connecting line joins the loop of the next cursive e (7), and when the downstroke below the loop is eliminated or almost eliminated, and when the concave, horizontal, final stroke is similar in form and size to the downstroke of the ''h'' and the following connecting line,

350

these are SPIDERS and the writer is very smart in handling people, can win them by charm and affability and like a spider can get them into his web.

When in the cursive h (6) the second part of the letter is reduced at the top, does not reach the baseline and the final downstroke is not parallel to slant of the initial downstroke, and when the following cursive e (7) is taller than the second part of the "h,"

351

these letters resemble the GREEK THETA and the writer is a perfect showman, can talk of matters of which he has but little knowledge so convincingly that people are impressed and believe him to be an expert in the particular field or subject.

When in the cursive h (6) the second part of the letter consists of a straight upstroke forming an angle with the straight, left slanting downstroke which in turn forms an angle with a short, straight connecting line joining the first downstroke of the next cursive n (6) which is pointed at the top and at the bottom, straight, reduced at the top, and slants to the left,

352

these are PYRAMIDS, ONE LARGE, ONE SMALL and the writer has the tendency to misrepresent facts and finds it difficult to distinguish between truth and fiction.

Chapter 22

LETTERS OF THE ALPHABET RESEMBLING
PICTORIAL FORMS: LETTERS "I" AND "i"

When in the Foreign I (4) the final curve ends with an indirect horizontal loop,

353

this is a LEFT TENDING ADDITIONAL LOOP and the writer cleverly hides malicious and perfidious designs.

When in the cursive I (4) or Foreign I (5) the final curve is convex, horizontal or slants upwards,

354

these are REVERSED STROKES and the writer while enjoying the reputation as a man of fine character, would not hesitate to slander a person.

When in the cursive I (4), after the initial upstroke of the complete or incomplete loop is made, the downstroke is generously convex, and when the final curve crosses the upstroke either in the upper or in the lower half,

355

these are PRETZELS and the writer can keep others in the dark about his true nature so that it will be difficult for them to figure him out.

When the cursive I (1) begins with the downstroke ending in a loop, which is out of proportion, and has a short, slightly downward slanting, final stroke which is not at level with the initial downstroke,

356

this is an INFANT and the writer pretends helplessness to arouse the sympathy of others and assure their aid.

When in the cursive I (1) the final stroke, which may be straight, touches or crosses the upstroke,

357

these are ROW BOATS and the writer dislikes committing himself and will cleverly extricate himself from situations which burden him with too much responsibility.

When the cursive I (1) begins with a small indirect loop at the top followed by the full downcurve ending in a horizontal loop, and when a short final stroke crosses the preceding downcurve,

358

this is the NUMBER 2 and the writer craves money and possessions so intensely that he would do anything in his power to acquire them.

When in the printed I (3) the two bars, which have almost the same length, are longer than the downstroke, and when the upper bar is convex and longer on the left side and the lower bar is concave and longer on the right side,

359

this is a BROKEN SLEIGH and the writer seeks to gain his ends by trickery.

When in the cursive I (4) the crossing of the loop, which begins with a convex, left tending downcurve, is about one-third to one-fourth of the height of the final downstroke ending in a point,

360

these are SABERS LOWERED and the writer at the slightest provocation resorts to a downright aggressive and offensive attitude.

When the printed I (3) consists only of a generously concave downstroke which has a short curve at each end,

361

or when the printed i (7) consists only of a generously concave down-stroke,

362

these are BRACKETS and the writer would not hesitate to use forceful means to control others.

When the downstroke of the printed i (7) is indicated only by two periods,

363

or when in the printed I (3) the downstroke is indicated only by a period,

364

these are STEMS resembling a PUNCTUATION MARK and the writer extricates himself from situations which burden him with too much re-sponsibility.

When the straight initial upstroke of the cursive i (6) is slightly retraced by the straight downstroke ending in a point at the baseline,

365

this is a DAGGER BLADE and the writer by using pressure and intimida-tion tries to force people into his services.

When in the cursive i (6) the downstroke is decidedly concave and slants to the left followed by a horizontal connecting line joining the next cursive e (7), and when the downstroke below the loop is almost elimi-nated and the slightly upward slanting connecting line joining the next cursive s (7) is similar in length to the preceding downstroke and the fol-lowing connecting line,

366

this is a SPIDER and the writer is very smart in handling people, can win them by charm and affability, and, like a spider, can get them into his web.

When in the consecutive cursive letters ih (6) one of the letters is higher than the other,

367

this is an UNUSABLE SURGICAL INSTRUMENT and the writer is shrewd and crafty and uses all sorts of tricks and schemes to gain his ends.

When the downstroke of the cursive i (6) slants to the left, the following cursive l (6) or the looped t (5) slants to the right, and when the back of and the downstrokes below the loops are concave and the letters have final strokes,

368

these are UNUSABLE ANCHORS and the writer feels insecure, is irresolute, vacillating in his opinion, not steadfast in purpose, and will frequently change his course of action.

When in the cursive "in" (6) or "im" (6) the downstrokes of the "n" or "m" are pointed and reduced at the top, round at the bottom, and do not reach the baseline, and when the intermediate strokes are longer than the height of the downstrokes which slant to the left and form angles with the connecting lines and intermediate strokes,

369

these are MOUNTAINS AND VALLEYS and the writer by resorting to boasting, bragging, and exaggerating seeks to impress and influence others.

When in the cursive "in" (6), after the initial upstroke is made, the following downstrokes slant in different directions, are short, alternately round or pointed at the top and at the bottom, are not aligned, and do not reach the baseline, and when the intermediate strokes are longer than the height of the downstrokes and the final stroke is almost horizontal,

370

these are CLOUDS and the writer is given to bluff, elaboration, and exaggeration to convince others of his own importance.

When the cursive i (6) begins with the downstroke forming a narrow curve with a short connecting line, and when the latter joins the first downstroke of the next cursive n (6) which is pointed and reduced at the top, does not reach the baseline, slants to the left, and curves into the intermediate stroke,

371

this is a PROFILE WITH BOWED HEAD and the writer at times is so ill-humored that he vents his spleen on others.

When the cursive i (6) begins with a long, almost straight downstroke forming a narrow curve with a long, straight connecting line joining the convex downstroke of the next cursive s (8) which is reduced at the top and ends above the baseline,

372

this is a SWAN and the writer uses all sorts of tricks and schemes to impress people and interest them for his plans.

When the connecting line between the cursive "is" (6, 8) curves into the convex downstroke of the succeeding "s", and when the horizontal final curve of the latter crosses the connecting line and joins the tip of the "i,"

373

this is a CHESS PAWN and the writer has the tendency to vex, humiliate, and subdue people.

When the downstroke of the cursive i (6) does not reach the baseline, and when the connecting line, which curves into the convex downstroke of the next cursive s (8) is longer than the height of the preceding letter,

374

these are DOUBLE HOOKS and the writer grasps every opportunity to succeed even at the expense of others.

When in the cursive "is" (6, 8) the long, straight, almost horizontal connecting line between the letters forms an angle with the downstroke of the "i" and curves into the convex downstroke of the "s" which is greater in width than in height,

375

this is a WHIP ON GROUND and the writer has the tendency to force his will upon others.

Chapter 23

LETTERS OF THE ALPHABET RESEMBLING PICTORIAL FORMS: LETTERS "J" AND "j"

When in the cursive J (1) the downstroke below the line curves into a horizontal stroke ending in an indirect loop,

376

this is a LEFT TENDING ADDITIONAL LOOP BELOW THE LINE and the writer can be vengefully malevolent.

When the cursive J (1) consists of two similar loops which are in horizontal position and greater in width than in height, and when the loops have a decidedly convex back and the upstroke of the lower loop partly retraces the initial upstroke and crosses the back of the loops,

377

this is a TULIP and the writer uses guile and trickery to deceive people.

When in the cursive J (1) the upper and the lower loops, which have a convex back, are inflated, and when the upstroke of the lower loop crosses the initial upstroke and the back of the upper loop above the baseline,

378

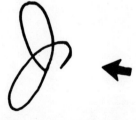

this is a PRETZEL and the writer can keep others in the dark about his true nature.

When in the cursive J (1) the upper and the lower loops, which have convex back, are inflated, and when the upstroke of the lower loop partly

116

retraces the initial upstroke at the baseline,

379

these are UNUSABLE PROPELLER BLADES and the writer lacks force, drive, and initiative.

When the cursive J (1) consists of a convex downstroke which has a short curve at each end, and when the following printed o (6) touches the downstroke almost in the center,

380

this is a POT COVER and the writer wants to have his way, under all circumstances enforce his will, and becomes stubborn and unreasonable when his demands are resisted or denied.

When the cursive j (6) consists of a straight downstroke forming an angle with a straight left tending, upward slanting stroke which in turn forms an angle with a right tending, horizontal, final stroke ending on the downstroke,

381

this is a TRIANGLE BELOW THE LINE and the writer uses underhanded and cruel means to weaken and control others.

When in the cursive J (1) the lower loop, which may be pointed and is much longer and slants more to the right than the upper one, has a convex back and a straight or almost straight upstroke,

382

this is a SINKING ROW BOAT and the writer when his patience dwindles and his zeal cools, will turn his back on all his responsibility.

When the cursive J (1) is loopless and begins with the downstroke forming a narrow curve with an upstroke at the right side, and when the latter is almost straight, at least half the height of and does not join the downstroke,

383

or when the cursive j (6) begins with the downstroke, and when the upstroke of the lower loop ends before it crosses the downstroke,

384

these are WHIPS HELD DOWN and the writer has the tendency to subjugate and tyrannize people.

When the bar of the printed J (2), which does not join the downstroke, is longer than the height of the downstroke which has a long horizontal curve at the baseline ending in a short curve turned up,

385

this is a RIDING CROP ON A PLANE and the writer wants to be the focus of interest, exert influence on people, and control them.

When in the Foreign J (5) the downstroke ends in a point below the line, and when the upstroke of the lower loop widens at the end, turns to the right before it reaches the baseline, and curves into the next letter "o," and when one of the letters is higher than the other,

386

these are LARGE SHEARS and the writer is callous and ruthless in pursuing his aims.

    When the cursive J (1) begins with a concave horizontal curve above the line followed by a short, oblong, ink-filled loop at the top of the downstroke, and when the latter slants in vertical direction and ends in a point below the line,

387

this is the REAR VIEW OF A BODY and the writer keeps his own counsel and successfully conceals his innermost thoughts and feelings.

    When in the Foreign J (5) the loop below the line is extremely large,

388

this is an INFLATED LOOP and the writer resorts to bluff to be better able to control others.

    When in the cursive j (6) the downstroke is convex and the upstroke of the short and narrow lower loop crosses the downstroke before it reaches the baseline and ends at level with the tip of it,

389

this is a SHEAF OF GRAIN and the writer has an uncanny ability to adapt himself to people, to speak their language and to ingratiate himself so artfully with them that they believe he is on their side.

    When the initial upstroke of the cursive j (7) ends in a short, oblong loop which slants to the right, and when the downstroke below the line slants in vertical direction and ends in a point,

390

this is a BODY WITH HEAD BENT FORWARD and the writer by subservience and apparent devotion gives the impression of completely agreeing with the ideas and wishes of people in order to better achieve his
aims.

    When the upstroke of the cursive j (6) is straight or almost straight,
and when the downstroke is short and ends in a point below the line,

391

this is a WEDGE and the writer is liable to sow discord and foment strife.

Chapter 24

LETTERS OF THE ALPHABET RESEMBLING PICTORIAL FORMS: LETTERS "K" AND "k"

When in the cursive K (2), after the downstroke is made, the second part of the letter consists of two convex downstrokes,

392

or when in the cursive K (2), after the downstroke is made, the second part of the letter consists of a convex downstroke and a concave horizontal stroke which join the downstroke at different points,

393

or when the cursive K (2) has a convex downstroke, and when the second part of the letter stands alone,

394

these are HORNS and the writer can become very obstinate and stubborn and will insist upon carrying out his ideas regardless of opposition and consequences.

When in the cursive K (1), after the initial downstroke is made, a convex first downstroke follows ending in a loop, which is out of proportion, and touches or crosses the initial downstroke, and when the second downstroke in turn is convex and shorter or longer than the first one,

395

this is an INFANT WITH HEAD AGAINST THE WALL and the writer when he has set his mind on something, is inclined to run his head against the wall and act without rhyme or reason.

When the second part of the cursive K (1) stands alone and has a convex first downstroke and a center loop, which is out of proportion, and when the following second downstroke is shorter or longer than the first one,

396

these are INFANTS and the writer pretends helplessness to arouse the sympathy of others and secure their aid.

When the second part of the cursive K (2), which stands alone, has a long, first downstroke which forms an angle with a short, straight, left tending upstroke, and when the upstroke in turn forms an angle with the concave, final downstroke which is drawn around the initial downstroke,

397

this is an AUTO GEAR SHIFT and the writer is an autocratic person who insists on having his own will, seeks to curb and limit others, and does not easily allow them to speak their mind.

When in the second part of the printed K (3) the first and the second downstroke are convex, and when both strokes are longer than the initial downstroke which they slightly cross,

398

this is a TENT and the writer is looking for thrills and sensations to overcome his feelings of loneliness, restlessness and frustration.

When the cursive K (1) begins with a short hook to the left and a straight downstroke follows which stands alone and ends with a short hook turned up to the right,

399

these are BRACKETS and the writer would not hesitate to use forceful means to control others.

When in the cursive K (2), or printed K (3, 4), after the initial downstroke is made, an upstroke, which may be concave and may have the same length as or be longer than the preceding downstroke, slightly retraces the downstroke at the baseline,

400 $\qquad$ *K* $\qquad$ *K* $\qquad$ *K*

these are INSERTS and the writer always finds something to object to, to criticize, and to reproach.

When the second part of the cursive K (2) stands alone and begins with a short upcurve followed by the first downcurve ending in an almost horizontal stroke which curves into a short downstroke,

401 $\qquad$ *k*

or when in the cursive K (2) the lower downstroke of the second part stands alone and consists of a vertical double curve ending in a horizontal stroke,

402 $\qquad$ *k*

these are DEMONIAC PROFILES OF NOSES and the writer enjoys creating confusion and dissension, using schemes and plots so cunningly that no one holds him responsible.

When the second part of the cursive K (2) stands alone and consists of a straight downstroke which forms an angle with a convex downcurve,

403 $\qquad$ *k*

or when the first downstroke of the cursive K (2) is slightly retraced by a downward slanting, convex curve which ends below the baseline,

404

these are PROFILES OF NOSES WITH WIDE NOSTRILS and the writer has malicious joy in surreptitiously inflicting injury.

When the second part of the cursive K (2) stands alone and consists of a convex downstroke which is slightly retraced by a double curve ending below the baseline,

405 $\qquad$ *k*

this is a PROFILE OF PUG NOSE and the writer is prone to vex and humiliate others by sarcastical and cynical remarks.

When in the second part of the cursive K (2), which stands alone, the first downstroke is long, straight and curves into a short, right tending, almost horizontal stroke curving into a left slanting, concave downcurve followed by the final upstroke,

406

this is a PROFILE OF NOSE WITH RECEDING CHIN and the writer pretends to acquiesce but will not live up to expectations.

When the second part of the cursive k (7) has a straight downstroke forming an angle with a short, straight, right tending, almost horizontal stroke, which in turn forms an angle with a concave downcurve followed by a horizontal final stroke,

407

this is a PROFILE OF NOSE WITH PROTRUDING CHIN and the writer knows how to find the Achilles tendon in people and to attack them in their vulnerable spots.

When in the cursive k (7) the crossing of the loop is low and the downstroke below the loop, which is short, is very close to the starting point of the initial upstroke,

408

this is a CLUB and the writer enforces his will on others.

When in the printed k (9), after the downstroke is made, a horizontal stroke crosses it in the lower half and ends in a double curve which is parallel to slant of the downstroke,

409

this is a DEVIL'S FORK and the writer under the mask of kindness and service, can cause all kinds of difficulties and confusion.

When the downstroke of the cursive k (8) slightly retraces the initial upstroke, which may be straight or curved, and when the second part of the letter does not reach the baseline,

410

these are DAGGER BLADES and the writer by using pressure and intimidation tries to force people into his services.

When in the cursive K (2) the second part of the letter stands alone and consists of an asymetrical double curve,

411

this is a GROVELING SNAKE and the writer can be friendly towards a person one day and betray him the next.

Chapter 25

LETTERS OF THE ALPHABET RESEMBLING PICTORIAL FORMS: LETTERS "L" AND "l"

When in the printed L (3), after the downstroke is made, a short retrace stroke follows and a concave, left slanting, downward slanting or horizontal curve which does not reach the baseline,

412

these are SHARP BEAKS and the writer seeks to provoke others by pointing out their shortcomings and reproaching them for them.

When the cursive L (2) starts with a convex downstroke ending in a small, open or ink-filled loop which is almost parallel to slant of the downstroke, and when a short, straight, downward slanting, final stroke follows,

413

these are DULL BEAKS and the writer is callous and ruthless in pursuing his aims.

When the cursive L (2) has a convex downstroke followed by a loop, which is out of proportion, and a short final stroke which is not at level with the preceding downstroke,

414

these are INFANTS and the writer pretends helplessness to arouse the sympathy of others and assure their aid.

When in the printed L (3) the downstroke, which slants to the right, and the bar, which slants slightly upwards, have almost the same length,

415

this is a WEDGE and the writer is liable to sow discord and foment strife.

When in the cursive L (1) the upper and the lower loop, which are different in form and size, slant almost in the same direction, and when the lower loop has an upward slanting, final stroke,

416

these letters resemble the GERMAN SCRIPT h (9) and the writer can exert influence on and take advantage of people.

When the printed L (3) has a long downstroke followed by a short retrace stroke and an upward slanting, concave bar,

417

this is a SCYTHE and the writer is ruthless and unscrupulous.

When the downstroke of the printed L (3) is slightly concave and curves into a bar which consists of a double curve,

418

this is a PROFILE OF NOSE WITH WIDE NOSTRILS and the writer has malicious joy in surreptitiously inflicting injury.

When the downstroke of the printed L (3) is convex,

419

this is a PROFILE OF PUG NOSE and the writer is prone to vex and humiliate others by sarcastic and cynical remarks.

When the cursive L (2) starts with a short, concave upcurve to the right, which in turn curves into a convex, left slanting downcurve ending below the baseline,

420

or when the printed L (3) begins with a short, concave upcurve followed by the downstroke forming an angle with a convex, downward slanting bar, which ends below the baseline,

421

these are DEMONIAC PROFILES OF NOSES and the writer enjoys creating confusion and dissension, using schemes and plots so cunningly that no one holds him responsible.

When in the cursive L (2) or L (1) , after a long downstroke is made, a left tending, slightly concave, upward slanting stroke forms an angle with a concave or straight, final stroke which crosses the downstroke,

422

these are PLIERS and the writer will try to attain his goal by forcible means.

When the cursive L (1) has a long, straight upstroke which is slightly retraced by a straight downstroke ending in a loop, and when the latter is parallel to slant of the downstroke and may have a short, straight, final stroke, if any,

423

or when the first loop of two consecutive cursive l's (6) has no initial upstroke and the downstroke below the loop ends in a point, and when a straight connecting line joins the shorter loop of the second "l" which is reduced at the top, does not reach the baseline, and may have a horizontal final stroke, if any,

424

these are BELLOWS and the writer is a show off and to reach his objective resorts to all sorts of tricks and ruses.

When in the cursive l (6) the downstroke below the loop extends below the baseline, curves to the left at the end, and narrows to a point,

425

this is an ALGA and the writer can give the impression of agreement and cooperation but seeks to accomplish his purpose by underhanded practice.

When in the cursive l (6) the loop has a concave back and the crossing is low, and when the final stroke, which is almost identical with the initial stroke, ends in a point at the baseline,

426

this is a FISH and the writer is so callous that he can become ruthless.

When in the cursive l (6) the downstroke below the loop narrows to a point and extends below the baseline,

427

or when the downstroke of the printed l (7) narrows to a point,

428

these are STINGS OF A WASP and the writer is given to bickering and provokes, criticizes and belittles others.

When in the cursive l (6) the initial upstroke is long and partly retraced by a long, concave downstroke which slants to the left at the end and ends at the baseline,

429

this is the EIFFEL TOWER and there are no limits to this writer's striving for power and his desire to gain the ascendency.

When the cursive l (6) slants to the right and the upstroke slants into the pointed top which is slightly retraced by the concave back of the loop, and when the crossing of the latter is low and the downstroke below the loop turns to the right at the point where the crossing ends,

430

this is a CANDLE WITH FLICKERING FLAME and the writer is apt to change his attitude towards his world unexpectedly and become disloyal.

When in the cursive l (6) the initial upstroke is eliminated and the loop is pointed, and when the downstroke below the loop is straight and ends in a point at the baseline,

431

this is a KNIFE HELD UP and the writer is envious and revengeful.

When in the cursive l (6), after the upstroke and the loop are made, the downstroke below the loop is straight and ends in a point, and when the short, straight, final stroke and the short, straight, initial upstroke have almost the same length and slant in the same direction,

432

this is an UNUSABLE ANCHOR and the writer feels insecure, is irresolute, vacillating in his opinion, not steadfast in purpose, and will frequently change his course of action.

When the printed l (7) begins with a short upcurve,

433

this is a RIDING CROP HELD UP and the writer tries to force people into his services.

When in the cursive l (6) the initial upstroke is almost eliminated, the loop is inflated and the downstroke below the loop ends in a point at the baseline,

434

these are WHIPS HELD UP and the writer exercises authority to have mastery of people or situations.

When the printed l (7) has a hook or curve at each end, at the right side of the downstroke,

435

this is a BRACKET and the writer would not hesitate to use forceful means to control others.

When the cursive l (6) begins with a concave downstroke followed by a rather short connecting line joining the succeeding cursive e (7) which may be at level with or higher than the preceding downstroke,

436

these are NUMBERS 6 IN LETTERS and the writer craves money and possessions so intensely that he would do anything in his power to acquire them.

When in the cursive lef (6, 7) the "l," which consists of a downstroke only, forms a narrow curve with the connecting line joining the succeeding "e," and when the latter has a narrow, ink-filled loop followed by a slightly concave, final stroke which extends far below the baseline, ends in a point and forms the downstroke of the "f," and when the upstroke of the "f," which is straight, slightly retraces the preceding downstroke and ends in a point above the baseline,

437

these are CENSURING FINGERS and the writer has the tendency to expose the imperfection of others and to reproach their shortcomings.

When in two consecutive, loopless, cursive l's (6) the downstrokes retrace the upstrokes to a great extent, and when the downstroke of the second letter extends below the baseline and ends in a point,

438

these are GRASPING FINGERS and the writer quickly takes advantage of any and every opportunity which will benefit him.

When in the cursive ley (6, 7) the l-loop has a concave back and the downstroke below the loop turns in horizontal direction at the point where the crossing, which is low, ends, and when the loop of the "y" is shorter than the preceding e-loop,

439

this is a SPRING and the writer by indulging in boasting and exaggeration seeks to impress people.

When in the cursive lf (6, 7) or 11 (6) the upper loops, which have concave backs and join almost in the middle, are inflated and cross low, and when the second loop is taller than the first one,

440

these are FLOWER PETALS and the writer grasps every opportunity to succeed even at the expense of others.

When the loops of two consecutive cursive l's (6) are narrow and nearly touch each other in the middle or at the top,

441

these are ANTHERS and the writer tries to hide his feelings of inadequacy by being stubborn and rejecting suggestions and/or propositions from the start.

When in the cursive 1 (6) the back of the loop is decidedly convex and ends at the starting point of the initial stroke,

442

this is a MELANCHOLY MOON and the writer has times of indifference and lack of interest when he is cool, icy and uncooperative.

Chapter 26

LETTERS OF THE ALPHABET RESEMBLING PICTORIAL FORMS: LETTERS "M" AND "m"

When the initial stroke of the cursive M (1) is long, slightly convex, left tending, and slightly retraced by a convex, right tending stroke which curves into the first downstroke, and when the latter joins the starting point of the initial stroke,

443

this is a FISH OF PREY and the writer makes such a guileless impression that people think him to be a most unselfish person, whereas in reality he will grasp every opportunity to take advantage of them.

When the downstroke of the cursive M (1), which is much longer than the rest of the letter, begins with a slightly convex downcurve, and when the last downstroke, which is straight, ends in a point at the baseline,

444

this is a GIRAFFE and the writer pretends to be interested in others but since he is only curious, it does not mean that he would make any special effort in their behalf.

When in the printed M (4), after the downstroke is made, a concave, downward slanting stroke follows which is longer than the height of the preceding and following downstroke and joins the tip of the short, final downstroke,

445

these are WEBBED FINGERS and the writer is skilled at tricking others and employs many a clever stratagem for reasons of self-protection.

When in the cursive M (2) the first downstroke forms an angle with the first intermediate stroke, which is straight, short, slants slightly upwards and in turn forms an angle with the second downstroke, and when the latter, which is greatly reduced at the top, forms an angle with the second intermediate stroke which is straight, short, and slants slightly upwards,

446

or when in the cursive M (2) the second downstroke, which is pointed at the top and does not reach the baseline, forms an angle with the second intermediate stroke, and when the latter is short and in turn forms an angle with the third downstroke, which is even shorter, greatly reduced at the top and at the bottom, and curves into a long, slightly convex upstroke,

447

these are POINTED FINGERS and the writer would not hesitate to coerce people into submission.

When in the cursive M (2) the first downstroke is pointed at the top and partly round at the bottom followed by an intermediate stroke which is retraced to some extent by the second downstroke, and when the latter is partly round at the bottom, reduced at the top, does not reach the baseline and followed by the second intermediate stroke,

448

these are AUTHORITATIVE FINGERS and the writer has the tendency to browbeat and humiliate others.

When in the Foreign M (5) the almost straight, initial upstroke is retraced to a great extent followed by a concave horizontal curve, and when the second downstroke partly retraces the upstroke of the preceding curve,

449

or when in the printed M (4) the initial upstroke is partly retraced, followed by a concave, horizontal curve, and when the second downstroke partly retraces the upstroke of the preceding curve,

450

or when in the cursive M (1) the first downstroke is pointed at the top
followed by the intermediate and the second downstroke which is greatly
reduced at the top and does not reach the baseline, and when the second
intermediate stroke joins the second downstroke which is pointed at the
top,

451

these are GRASPING FINGERS and the writer very quickly takes advantage of any and every opportunity.

When in the cursive M (1), after the first downstroke and the first
intermediate stroke are made, the second downstroke does not reach the
baseline, and when the following second intermediate stroke slightly
retraces and extends far above the preceding downstroke and curves into
the third downstroke ending in a point,

452

these are GUIDING FINGERS and the writer is self-opinionated, convinced of his own wisdom and knows that his advice is the best that can
be given.

When in the cursive M (2) the first downstroke is pointed at the top
followed by the first intermediate stroke extending far above the preceding downstroke, and when the following humps are pointed and the second
downstroke, which is longer than the preceding, does not reach the baseline, and when the third downstroke, which is shorter than the second one,
ends in a point,

453

or when in the cursive M (2), after the first intermediate and the second downstroke are made, the second intermediate stroke extends above the preceding downstroke which is pointed at the top and extends below the baseline,

454

or when the first or the second downstroke of the printed M (4) is longer than the other,

455

these are WARNING FINGERS and the writer tries to gain the upper hand by intimidation and force.

When the third part of the cursive M (2) stands alone,

456

this is a DEMONIAC PROFILE OF NOSE and the writer enjoys creating confusion and dissension, using schemes and plots so cunningly that no one holds him responsible.

When the second downstroke of the cursive M (1), which does not reach the baseline, forms an angle with a short, right tending, almost horizontal intermediate stroke, and when the latter forms an angle with a concave, horizontal curve which does not reach the baseline,

457

this is a PROFILE OF POINTED NOSE and the writer can become extremely sarcastic and cynical and will not easily admit a single good quality in others.

When in the cursive M (2) the downstrokes, the intermediate strokes, and the humps are different in form, size, and slant,

458

these are MIXED ARCHITECTURAL STYLES and the writer is a perfect showman, can talk of matters of which he has but little knowledge so convincingly that people are impressed and believe him to be an expert in the particular field or subject.

When in the cursive M (2) the initial upstroke is straight and slightly retraced by the first downstroke which slants to the left, and when the first intermediate stroke crosses the preceding downstroke in the lower half and is slightly retraced by the second downstroke which slants to the left,

459

this is a HERALDIC SYMBOL and the writer seeks to impress his world as trustworthy and reliable by pretending to be punctillious about conventions.

When the cursive M (2) starts high above the baseline with a long, slightly undercurved initial upstroke which forms an angle with a straight, left slanting, second downstroke, and when the space between the upstroke and the second downstroke is at least as wide as or wider than the height of the strokes,

460

this is a TENT and the writer is looking for thrills and sensations to overcome his feelings of loneliness, restlessness and frustration.

When the initial upstroke of the cursive M (1) begins halfway, is concave, and curves into the first downstroke which is much longer than the rest of the letter,

461

this is a WHIP HELD UP and the writer exercises authority to have mastery of people or situations.

When in the cursive M (2) the first downstroke is pointed at the top followed by the first intermediate stroke, which partly retraces it, ends in a point, and may be shorter than or have the same length as the preceding downstroke,

462

this is an INSERT and the writer always finds something to object to, to criticize, and to reproach.

When the Foreign M (5) begins below the baseline with a large e-loop followed by a long upstroke,

463

this is a STONE and the writer can make difficulties for others and put obstacles in their way so furtively that he cannot easily be held responsible.

When in the cursive M (1), after the final downstroke is made, a long, initial upstroke of any following letter crosses it,

464

this is a DIAGONAL CROSSING and the writer can create strife and confusion and seriously interfere with the plans of others.

When in the cursive M (2) the slightly concave, initial upstroke begins at the baseline and is slightly retraced by the first downstroke which is round at the bottom, much longer than the rest of the letter, and does not reach the baseline,

465

this is a TOWER and the writer can harass, embarrass, and infuriate people so that they lose their self-confidence enabling him to impose his will.

When the last downstroke of the Foreign M (5) is concave, entends far below the baseline and may or may not end in a curve turned up to the right,

466

or when the final downstroke of the cursive m (6), which may be straight, ends in a point or in a curve turned up to the right and extends far below the baseline,

467

these are ALGAE and the writer gives the impression of agreement and cooperation but seeks to accomplish his purpose by underhanded practice.

When in the printed M (4) the final downstroke slants to the left, or when the initial downstroke slants to the right and the final downstroke slants to the left,

468

or when in the cursive m (7) the second and third downstrokes, which slant to the left, are pointed at the top and form angles with the preceding and following straight intermediate strokes, and when the second downstroke, which ends high above the baseline, is greatly reduced at the top and at level with the third downstroke ending in a point at the baseline,

469

these are CROWNS and the writer pretends to acknowledge the superiority of others, but actually wants to have the reins in his own hand, and he tries to attain this control by employing many a clever stratagem or effectual force.

When in the cursive M (2) the downstrokes are pointed and gradually reduced at the top, and when the first intermediate stroke forms angles with the preceding and following downstrokes, and when the second downstroke ends in a curve high above the baseline followed by a short, second intermediate stroke which is slightly retraced by the third downstroke ending in a point below the baseline,

470

(this is the NUMBER 14)

or when the final downstroke of the cursive M (2) is longer than the preceding strokes, pointed at the top and does not reach the baseline, and
when the succeeding cursive e (7) may be higher than or at level with the
preceding downstroke,

471

(this is the NUMBER 6)

or when the cursive m (7) or M (2) begins with a concave.downstroke
ending in a curve followed by a loop, which is greatly reduced at the top,
and may be higher than or at level with the preceding downstroke,

472

(this is the NUMBER 6)

or when the cursive m (6) begins with a short, concave upcurve followed
by the first downstroke which is slightly retraced by the first, straight,
intermediate stroke, and when the second downstroke is pointed at the top
and ends in a concave curve high above the baseline, and when the third
downstroke is straight, reduced at the top, retraces the end of the preceding curve, and ends in a point below the line,

473

(this is the NUMBER 24)

these are NUMBERS IN LETTERS and the writer craves money and possessions so intensely that he would do anything in his power to acquire
them.

When the humps of the printed m (8) are flat and the space between
is greater than the height of the downstrokes, and when the initial upstroke, if any, is horizontal and at level with the humps,

474

these are ELEPHANTS and the writer is unwilling to cooperate, cannot be
forced and wants to have his own way.

When in the cursive m (6, 7) the initial upstroke curves into the
first downstroke, which is convex and curves to the left at the end, forming

an indirect loop with a concave upstroke crossing near the top, and when
the second hump and a convex, second downstroke follow,

475

this is a SPIDER and the writer is very smart in handling people, can win
them by charm and affability, and like a spider can get them into his web.

When the third part of the cursive m (6) stands alone and begins
with a short, concave upcurve followed by a downstroke and an upward
slanting, straight or slightly concave, final stroke,

476

this is a SWAN and the writer uses all sorts of tricks and schemes to
impress people and interest them for his plans.

When the second hump of the cursive m (6, 7) is pointed,

477

these are ARCHITECTURAL STYLES and the writer feigns so much
sympathy and understanding that others believe him to be interested in
their well-being and ready to sacrifice, in reality he is callous and ruthless.

When in the cursive m (6) the first two downstrokes slant to the
left and are gradually reduced and pointed at the top, and when the initial
upstroke is straight and forms an angle with the first downstroke followed
by the straight, first intermediate stroke which in turn forms angles with
the preceding and the following downstrokes,

478

these are PYRAMIDS, ONE LARGE, ONE SMALL and the writer has the
tendency to misrepresent facts and finds it difficult to distinguish between
truth and fiction.

When the cursive m (7) is greater in height than in width and higher
than the preceding letter, and when the downstrokes are straight and
pointed at the top and at the bottom,

479

this is a PICKET FENCE and the writer is clever at shifting responsibility and letting others take the blame.

When the cursive m (7) is greater in width than in height, and when the downstrokes are short, vertical, pointed at the top and round at the bottom, and when the intermediate strokes which only slightly retrace the downstrokes, are almost horizontal,

480

these are COMBS and the writer can ruthlessly force people to comply with his wishes.

When the cursive m (6) consists of three identical "e's" which are close to each other,

481

these are COILS and the writer can win people by charm and affability so that they do not recognize his true nature.

When in the cursive m (6) the second downstroke, which does not reach the baseline, is slightly retraced by the second intermediate stroke, and when the latter in turn is slightly retraced by the third downstroke which is higher and slants in a different direction than the second downstroke,

482

these are CREVICES and the writer can disconcert, bewilder, and confuse people to gain control over them.

When in the cursive m (6), after the initial upstroke is made, the downstrokes are short, not aligned, slant to the left, end high above the baseline and are alternately round or pointed at the top and at the bottom, and when the intermediate strokes are longer than the height of the downstrokes and the final stroke is almost horizontal,

483

this is a CLOUD and the writer is given to bluff, elaboration and exaggeration to convince others of his importance.

When in the cursive m (7) the second intermediate stroke curves into the third, shorter downstroke which slants to the left and does not reach the baseline, and when the following cursive e (7) slants to the right and is taller than the last downstroke of the "m,"

484

these letters resemble the GREEK THETA t (8) and the writer is a perfect showman, can talk of matters of which he has but little knowledge so convincingly that people are impressed and believe him to be an expert in the particular field or subject.

When in the printed m (8) the center part does not reach the baseline,

485

this is a TOMB STONE and the writer by pretending to be a gentleman of the old school hopes to give the impression of being kind and unselfish.

When in the cursive m, n (6) the initial, the final, the intermediate strokes and the connecting lines form angles with the downstrokes at the top and at the bottom, and when they are about twice the height of the downstrokes,

486

this is a HACKSAW and the writer is callous and merciless.

Chapter 27

LETTERS OF THE ALPHABET RESEMBLING PICTORIAL FORMS: LETTERS "N" AND "n"

When the cursive N (1) begins with the downstroke followed by the intermediate stroke, the hump, and the last downstroke which is straight and ends in a point at the baseline,

487

these are GIRAFFES and the writer pretends to be interested in others but since he is only curious, it does not mean that he would make any special effort in their behalf.

When the printed N (3) begins with an upstroke curving into the center stroke, which is partly round at the bottom, and followed by a final upstroke which is concave and much longer than the preceding strokes,

488

or when the cursive N (1) consists of an incomplete, large, initial loop followed by the first downstroke, which ends in a curve and has a convex, final upstroke,

489

these are VIPERS and the writer can be so affable, kind, and obliging that everyone believes him friendly disposed and does not believe him capable of falsehood and deceit.

When in the cursive N (2) the first downstroke, which is longer at the bottom than the second one, is slightly retraced by the intermediate stroke, and when the latter curves into or is partly retraced by the second downstroke,

490

144

these are POINTED FINGERS and the writer would not hesitate to coerce people into submission.

When the first downstroke of the cursive N (2) forms a narrow curve with the intermediate stroke which is shorter than the preceding downstroke, and when the second downstroke slightly retraces the intermediate stroke and does not reach the baseline,

491

these are AUTHORITATIVE FINGERS and the writer has the tendency to browbeat and humiliate people.

When in the cursive N (2), after the initial stroke and the first downstroke are made, the following intermediate stroke extends high above the preceding strokes and is slightly retraced by the second downstroke which does not reach the baseline,

492

these are WARNING FINGERS and the writer tries to gain the upper hand by force and intimidation.

When in the printed N (3), after the first downstroke is made, the second downstroke is reduced at the top, and when the center stroke, which starts in the upper half of the first downstroke, crosses the second downstroke in the lower half,

493

this is a PASTURE GATE and the writer is prone to tyrannize others and to restrict them in their actions.

When in the cursive N (2) the initial upstroke is straight and slightly retraced by the first downstroke which slants to the left, and when the intermediate stroke crosses the preceding downstroke in the lower half, and is slightly retraced by the second downstroke which slants to the left, is straight, and ends in a point,

494

this is a HERALDIC SYMBOL and the writer tries to impress his world as trustworthy and reliable by pretending to be punctillious about conventions.

When the printed N (3) begins with a right slanting upstroke at the baseline followed by the center stroke and the final stroke which is short and slants to the right, and when the space between the initial and the center stroke is at least as wide as or wider than the height of the strokes,

495

this is a TENT and the writer is looking for thrills and sensations to over-come his feelings of loneliness, restlessness and frustration.

When the Foreign N (5) begins about halfway with a short, straight, left tending downstroke forming an angle with a slightly concave, up-stroke which in turn forms an angle with the second downstroke touching the starting point of the initial stroke,

496

this is a HATCHET and the writer resorts to force and pressure to attain his goal.

When in the printed N (3) the second part stands alone, and when, after the center stroke is made, the final upstroke follows which is longer than the preceding and slants to the right,

497

this is an INSERT and the writer always finds something to object to, to criticize, and to reproach.

When in the printed N (3), after the first downstroke is made, the rest of the letter stands alone and consists of a concave center stroke followed by a final downstroke which joins or crosses the end of the pre-ceding stroke,

498   14

(this is the NUMBER 14)

or when in the cursive n (6) the straight, initial upstroke forms an angle with a concave, left slanting, first downstroke which is round at the base-line, and when an intermediate stroke follows forming an angle with the second, almost straight downstroke, which is parallel to the preceding downstroke, extends below the baseline, and ends in a point,

499

(this is the NUMBER 4)

these are NUMBERS IN LETTERS and the writer craves money and possessions so intensely that he would do anything in his power to acquire them.

When the final downstroke of the cursive N (2) is concave, extends below the baseline and ends in a point or in a short curve, turned up to the right,

500

these are ALGAE and the writer gives the impression of agreement and cooperation but seeks to accomplish his purpose by underhanded practice.

When the initial upstroke of the cursive N (2) is long and curves into the first downstroke which is much longer than the rest of the letter,

501

these are WHIPS HELD UP and the writer exercises authority to have mastery of people and situations.

When in the cursive n (6) the initial upstroke begins with a short, concave upcurve above the baseline, followed by the first downstroke which is much longer than the second one,

502

this is a RIDING CROP and the writer tries to force people into his services.

When the cursive n (6) consists of two identical "e's" which are close to each other,

503

this is a COIL and the writer can win people by charm and affability so that they do not recognize his true nature.

When the cursive n (6) has a long, convex, intermediate stroke which is retraced by the short, left slanting, second downstroke, and when the intermediate stroke is similar in form and dimension to the downstroke and the final stroke,

504

this is a SEA GULL and the writer devises secret and underhanded plans against the interest of those who trust him.

When the cursive n (6) begins with a slightly concave downstroke which curves into a short intermediate stroke forming an angle with the second downstroke, and when the latter is concave, slants to the left, and ends in a point below the line,

505

this is a PROFILE OF HOOKED NOSE and the writer can be friendly to one's face but at the same time harbor malicious and wicked designs.

When the cursive n (6) begins with a straight, first downstroke, and when a short, straight intermediate stroke in turn forms angles with both the first and the second straight, left slanting downstrokes, and when the second downstroke is reduced at the top and ends in a point at the baseline,

506

these are PYRAMIDS, ONE LARGE, ONE SMALL, and the writer has the tendency to misrepresent facts and finds it difficult to distinguish between truth and fiction.

When in the cursive n (6, 8) the straight initial upstroke forms an angle with the first downstroke, which is straight, slants to the left, ends high above the baseline and in turn forms an angle with the following straight intermediate stroke, and when the latter forms an angle with the second downstroke which is straight, slants to the left and ends in a point,

507

these are CROWNS and the writer pretends to acknowledge the superiority of others but actually wants to have the reins in his own hands and tries to attain this control by employing many a clever stratagem or force.

When the downstrokes of the printed n (7) consist of two broad consecutive periods,

508

these are STEMS resembling PUNCTUATION MARKS and the writer extricates himself from situations which burden him with too much responsibility.

When in the cursive N (2) the initial stroke is concave, slants down and to the left and curves into the first downstroke,

509

this is a BROAD PROFILE OF NOSE and the writer has malicious joy in belittling others and their achievements.

When the second downstroke of the cursive n (6) is concave, pointed at the top, slants to the left and does not reach the baseline, followed by a horizontal connecting line joining the succeeding cursive e (7), and when the downstroke below the loop is eliminated and the concave, horizontal, final stroke is similar in form and size to the downstroke of the preceding "n" and the following connecting line,

510

or when the second downstroke of the cursive n (6) is higher, pointed at the top, concave, slants to the left, followed by a horizontal connecting line joining the stubby loop of the next cursive 1 (6), and when the downstroke below the loop is eliminated and the concave and horizontal connecting line is similar to the last downstroke of the preceding "n" and the following connecting line,

511

or when in the cursive n (6) the initial upstroke curves into the first downstroke, which is convex, curves to the left at the end, and forms an indirect loop with a concave upstroke crossing near the top, and when the second hump and the second downstroke, which is convex and ends in a point, follow,

512

these are SPIDERS and the writer is very smart in handling people, can win them by charm and affability, and like a spider can get them into his web.

When the final downstroke of the cursive n (6) is pointed at the top, concave, does not reach the baseline, and curves into an almost horizontal connecting line which is longer than the height of the preceding and following letters, and when the connecting line curves into the succeeding cursive s (8), which consists of a convex downstroke only and ends below the baseline,

513

this is a DOUBLE HOOK and the writer grasps every opportunity to succeed even at the expense of others.

When horizontal strokes are substituted for small letters as in the cursive ''ng,''

514

these are WIRES and the writer hides his real intentions so skillfully that it will be difficult to discover what he is planning to do.

When in the cursive n (6) the last downstroke is pointed at the top, concave, shorter and higher than the preceding and followed by a long, almost horizontal, connecting line which joins the succeeding loop of the cursive l (6), and when the crossing of the loop is at level with the top of the second downstroke, and when the final stroke is eliminated or almost eliminated,

515

these are RECEDING FOREHEADS and the writer is narrow minded and intolerant.

Chapter 28

LETTERS OF THE ALPHABET RESEMBLING PICTORIAL FORMS: LETTERS "O" AND "o"

When in the cursive O (2), which is incomplete, the final upcurve is short, curves back to the baseline, and ends before reaching it,

516

or when the cursive o (5) is incomplete and has a short, final upcurve ending in a loop, and when the final stroke, if any, turns in horizontal direction at the point where the crossing ends,

517

these are NUMBERS 6 IN LETTERS and the writer craves money and possessions so intensely that he would do anything in his power to acquire them.

When the cursive o (5) has a wide opening at the top,

518

these are INCOMPLETE OVALS and the writer is a superficial observer who overlooks important details leading him to inaccurate conclusions.

When the cursive or printed "o" is circular and/or elliptical, free of inner loops and strokes,

519

these are CIRCLES and ELLIPSES and the writer is a quick thinker and has a good perceptive faculty.

When the cursive or printed "o" is circular and/or elliptical and the "a-oval" is not completed,

520

these are COMPLETE AND INCOMPLETE CIRCLES AND ELLIPSES and there is a great discrepancy between the writer's thinking and acting. He grasps things quickly but has neither the power of decision, the vigor nor the initiative to put his knowledge into action.

When in the cursive o (5), which is incomplete, the upcurve is longer than the initial downcurve and ends in a loop,

521

this is a BROKEN EGG SHELL and the writer pretends helplessness and inexperience so well that others come to his aid.

When the upcurve of the cursive o (5) crosses the downcurve near the top,

522

these are SMALL FISHES and the writer is so callous that he can become ruthless.

When the cursive o (5) is greater in width than in height and has a long, horizontal curve at the bottom,

523

these are PEARS and the writer at times feels listless, bored, and shows little interest in his world.

When the cursive o (5) is incomplete, the upcurve is longer than the initial downcurve and forms an angle with a long, straight, right tending, horizontal stroke,

524

this is a PELICAN and the writer tends to point out the weaknesses of others and by carping criticism undermines their self-confidence.

When in the cursive on (5, 6) the first downstroke of the "n" is round at the bottom, or when in the cursive on (5, 6), oo (5), ou (5, 6), ov (5), ow (5) the first letter, which may or may not be completed and/or may have a longer upcurve, curves into the downstroke of the second letter,

525

these are GLOSSY SNAKES and the writer can slyly extricate himself from unwelcome situations.

When the cursive o (5) begins above the baseline, is not completed, and the longer upcurve extends to the top of the loopless or looped cursive f (7) which slants in a different direction than the preceding letter,

526

these are ENCIRCLING ARMS and the writer devises underhanded plans so cunningly that others do not suspect him as the originator of their difficulties.

When the upcurve of the cursive o (5) or printed o (6) slightly retraces the initial downcurve and ends in a short, slightly concave downstroke extending into the oval,

527

these are CAT'S EYES and the writer gives the impression of being kind and lamb-like but can unexpectedly change this attitude and become unkind and antagonistic.

When two printed o's (6) are almost identical and close to each other,

528

these are CLOSE-SET EYES and the writer is a keen observer and draws sound deductions.

When the printed o (6) is not completed and the final stroke is above and beyond the initial stroke,

529

these are COCKATOO EYES and the writer is hypocritical in his demonstration of friendship and loyalty.

When the cursive o (5) begins and ends with an e-loop, and when both loops of different sizes join,

530

these are CUNNING EYES and the writer can adapt himself to others so adroitly that they think he is highly interested in them and take his words at face value, while in reality he has mental reservations.

When the cursive o (5), which is greater in width than in height, begins with a straight, horizontal stroke around which the oval is drawn and the final stroke begins at the end of the initial stroke,

531

this is an EYE OF THE CYCLOPS and the writer is shrewd and cunning, and although he does not miss a thing, he is successful in concealing his deductions.

When the cursive o (5) which may have a short final stroke, has an ink-filled loop inside the oval at the top,

532

these are EVASIVE EYES and the writer can be deceitful and disloyal.

When the cursive o (5) or printed o (6) shows every and any type of variation,

533

these are FLICKERING EYES and the writer's attitude is incalculable. He can be kind and likeable one day but ill-disposed and repulsive the next.

When the cursive o (5) is greater in width than in height and a narrow, oblong horizontal loop completes the oval,

534

this is an EYE-LID HALF CLOSED and the writer's interest in people must not deceive one into believing that he is unselfish and ready to sacrifice.

When in the cursive o (5) the width is greater than the height or vice versa, and when the incomplete oval begins with a convex upcurve and ends with an e-loop within the oval,

535

these are IRRESISTIBLE EYES and the writer exerts a fascinating influence on people and can win their affection, acceptance, and confidence.

When in the cursive o (5) or printed o (6) the upcurve extends above and beyond the starting point of the preceding downcurve, either to the left or parallel to slant,

536

or when in the cursive o (5) the upcurve slightly retraces the tip of the downcurve,

537

these are MONGOLIAN EYES and the writer can harass people until they yield to his wishes.

When the cursive o (5) ends with a loop which is half in and half outside the oval,

538

these are POPPING EYES and the writer conceals his selfish intentions by pretending to be both interested and sympathetic.

When the cursive o (5) or printed o (6) is so heavily inked that no white space or only little white space shows,

539

these are SINISTER EYES and the writer although manifesting feelings of friendship and loyalty, is capable of surreptitiously inflicting injury.

When in the cursive o (5), after the oval is made, the initial downcurve is retraced about half way, and when a final downcurve crosses the oval in the middle or almost in the middle,

540

these are SLY EYES and the writer conceals his true intentions so skillfully that others do not recognize them and are inclined to confide in him.

When the oval of the cursive o (5) begins with a period within the oval followed by a short, convex, initial upcurve and the downcurve, and when the final upcurve joins the initial upcurve,

541

these are SPARKLING EYES and the writer tries to gain the good graces of others by being so fascinating and alluring that he can control them.

When the initial downstroke of the cursive o (5) is long and forms a narrow curve with a shorter upcurve which does not join the downstroke and has a tick-out stroke,

542

these are AUTHORITATIVE FINGERS and the writer has the tendency to browbeat and humiliate others.

When the printed o (6) is not completed and narrows at the top,

543

this is a HORSESHOE and the writer has the tendency to limit and restrict others and to force his will on them.

When in the cursive o (5) the initial downstroke is longer than and forms a narrow curve with the upstroke which ends in a loop on the downstroke,

544

or when the cursive o (5), which has a narrow curve at the bottom, ends with a loop within the oval,

545

these are QUIVERS and the writer is bitterly vindictive.

When the cursive o (5) is not completed and begins with a short, straight upstroke which forms an angle with the initial downcurve, and when the upcurve is longer than the downcurve and ends in an oblong loop,

546

this is a FISH HOOK and the writer uses all kinds of tricks and ruses to gain the good graces of people planning to get something from them.

When the cursive o (5) starts above the baseline with a straight, almost horizontal initial stroke, which is retraced at the end, followed by an oval, which is greater in width than in height, and has a narrow curve at the right side,

547

this is a SPADE and the writer resorts to force and pressure to achieve his objective.

When the cursive o (5) or printed o (6) begins with a straight downstroke which forms angles with the upcurve,

548

this is a WAXING MOON and the writer is apt to change his attitude unexpectedly and become sarcastic, caustic, and acrimonious.

When in the cursive o (5) one side of the oval is straight or almost straight, the other arched,

549

these are PEBBLES and the writer is inordinately selfish and greedy.

When in two consecutive o's (5) and in the next cursive d (6) the ovals are deflated, the upcurves are longer than the preceding downcurves and form angles with the following straight connecting lines, and when the latter are longer than the height of the ovals and one connecting line is higher than the other,

550

these are COBBLE STONES and the writer is prone to vex and humiliate people by sarcastic and cynical remarks.

When the downcurve of the incomplete cursive o (5) ends in a point, and when the upcurve decidedly curves to the left and forms an angle with a straight, almost horizontal, connecting line which joins the succeeding

cursive c (6), and when the latter slightly retraces the preceding connecting line and does not reach the baseline,

551

this is an ANVIL and the writer resorts to ruthless and forcible means to
gain his ends.

When the longer upcurve of the complete or incomplete cursive o
(5) directly curves into the downstroke of the following cursive f (7) which
has a double curve and forms a complete or incomplete loop below the
line,

552

these are VENOMOUS SNAKES and the writer through charm, affability,
and diplomacy can win the acceptance of people so that they do not recognize his false nature.

When the cursive o (5) begins above the baseline with an almost
straight upstroke around which the oval is drawn, and when the following
connecting line joins the tip of the next cursive f (7) which has no loop
above the line,

553

or when the cursive o (5) begins with a short initial upstroke around
which the oval is drawn, and when the latter forms an angle with a long,
straight connecting line joining the next cursive n (6) which is higher,
slants more to the left than the preceding ''o'' and is pointed at the top,

and when the intermediate stroke is straight and forms angles with the second downstroke of the "n" which is reduced at the top and longer at the bottom than the first one,

554

these are RAILWAY TRAFFIC SIGNALS and the writer gives himself an air of importance by directing and guiding others and assuming the guise of a responsible and reliable person.

When in the cursive of (5, 7), after the "o" is made, the "f," which is parallel to the "o," has a narrow, open or ink-filled, upper loop and the downstroke ends in a point below the line, and when a left tending, final upstroke touches the upcurve of the preceding "o" or retraces the downstroke of the "f,"

555

these are AIRSHIPS GROUNDED and the writer resorts to all sorts of tricks and maneuvers for the effective staging of his plans.

When in the cursive of (5, 7), after the oval is made, the tick-out stroke directly curves into the top of the "f" which is parallel or almost parallel to the preceding "o" and has a much shorter downstroke above the line, and when the upstroke of the lower loop crosses the downstroke and joins or almost joins the bottom of the preceding "o",

556

these are SUBMARINES and the writer is so much concerned about safeguarding his own interests that he disregards those of others.

When in the cursive of (5, 7), after the oval is made, a short, straight, horizontal or almost horizontal connecting line forms an angle with the top of the "f," which is parallel or almost parallel to the preceding "o," has a much shorter downstroke above the line and ends in a point below the line,

557

these are GALLOWS WITH NOOSES and the writer can trick, trap, and outwit people.

When in the cursive oh (5, 6) the oval is incomplete and the upcurve extends above the downcurve and curves into the pointed, narrow or ink-filled loop of the following "h",

558

these are SHEARS and the writer is cruel and his machinations are at times harmful.

When the cursive o (5) is deflated and consists of a short down-stroke followed by an even longer upstroke which forms an angle with a straight, downward slanting, connecting line, and when the latter joins the tip of the next cursive i (6) which is reduced, at the top, slopes to the left, has a short final stroke, if any, and does not reach the baseline,

559

this is a TORPEDO BOAT and the writer is prone to complain, nag and find fault with others.

When in the cursive om (6) the oval is incomplete followed by a long connecting line forming an angle with the first downstroke of the next "m," and when the space between the two letters widens towards the bottom,

560

this is a SACRIFICIAL BLOCK and the writer can be cruel and callous.

When in the cursive o (5), after the oval is made, a slightly convex connecting line, which is longer than the height of the preceding "o," curves into the next cursive n (6) which ends in a point and has no final stroke,

561

this is a RHINOCEROS and the writer will record unpleasant and dis-turbing incidents.

When the upcurve of the incomplete cursive o (5) ends in a small loop followed by a short, connecting line curving into the first downstroke of the next cursive n (6) which slants to the left and curves into the intermediate stroke,

562

or when the longer upcurve of the incomplete cursive o (5) ends in a small
loop followed by the slant line which curves into the next cursive r (7),

563

these are BODIES LEANING BACK and the writer through charm and affability tries to shift responsibility.

When the cursive o (5) simply consists of an indirect oval, and when
the upcurve extends above the downcurve and joins the first downstroke
of the next cursive n (6) with a noticeably convex curve, and when the
rest of the letter is greatly reduced at the top,

564

this is a LANTERN and the writer is inclined to pose and show off in
order to impress his world.

When, after the cursive o (5) is made, a double curved connecting
line follows, which joins the first downstroke of the succeeding cursive
n (6), which does not reach the baseline,

565

this is a FOLDING MIRROR and the writer is practical, has a feeling for
the essentials and orders his life well.

When in the cursive o (5), after the oval is made, the tick is long,
and when the downstrokes of the following cursive n (6) slope to the left,
are pointed and/or partly round at the top and at the bottom and do not
reach the baseline, and when the last downstroke of the "n" is reduced
at the top and may or may not be longer at the bottom, and when the final
stroke is short or eliminated,

566

these are SHORT DRILLS and the writer is ruthless in pursuing his aims.

When the cursive o (5) is not completed and forms an angle with a
straight, short connecting line which in turn forms an angle with the first
downstroke of the next cursive n (6) which does not reach the baseline,

567

these are NUMBERS 5 LYING ON THE LINE and the writer tries to impress people by pretending to be highly interested in their well-being and
to be ready to extend himself for them.

When the connecting line or lines between two deflated cursive o's (5) or between them and the following deflated d-oval, are much longer than the height of the preceding letter,

568

these are MONUMENT CHAINS and the writer carefully weighs, investigates, and examines matters before he makes up his mind.

When two consecutive o's (5) are different in form and size and/or the second "o" is higher than the first one,

569

these are UNUSABLE EYE GLASSES and the writer is inquisitive, enjoys detecting the weak spots in others, and gossiping about them.

When in two consecutive cursive o's (5) and in a cursive d (6) the ovals slant in different directions, the o's have no tick and the connecting lines are straight,

570

these are DISKS ON A ROD and the writer's periodical interest in people and their problems cannot be taken seriously because there is a great discrepancy between his words and intentions.

When, after the cursive o (5) is made, a straight, horizontal, connecting line forms an angle with the straight, left slanting downstroke of the next cursive v (5, 6) or curves into the left slanting downstroke of the next cursive r (8), and when the last letters end in a point,

571

these are MASTER KEYS and the writer knows all the tricks necessary to hold his own and suavely and skillfully protects his own interests.

When the cursive o (5) has a long tick, and when the downstrokes of the following cursive rm (8, 6) are not retraced, slope to the left, are round at the top and at the bottom, and gradually shorter towards the end, and when the connecting lines and the intermediate strokes are longer than the height of the downstrokes, and when the final strokes are horizontal,

572

these are WEAK DRILLS and the writer is not very convincing and finds it difficult to arouse the interest of people for his plans.

Chapter 29

LETTERS OF THE ALPHABET RESEMBLING PICTORIAL FORMS: LETTERS "P" AND "p"

When the Foreign P (6) begins with the downstroke followed by a generous curve, which is drawn above and around it, and ends in a left tending downstroke or in a horizontal stroke crossing the downstroke near the top,

573

these are PRETZELS and the writer can keep others in the dark about his true nature so that it will be difficult for them to figure him out.

When in the printed P (4), after the downstroke is made, the indirect arc begins either at the right side, crosses and is drawn around it, or at the left side, is drawn around and crosses it,

574

these are STAGES WITH A PERSON IN THE FRONT and the writer is eager to stand in the limelight and is longing for recognition and acknowledgement.

When in the printed P (4), after the downstroke is made, the indirect arc begins above and is drawn around it, is longer on the right side and ends by crossing it near the top,

575

or when in the printed P (4), after the downstroke is made, the indirect arc begins above and is drawn around it, is longer on the left side and ends near the top,

576

these are STAGES WITH A PERSON ON THE SIDE and the writer wants to be the center of attraction but purposely places himself in the background to impress people as a modest and humble person.

When the cursive P (2) begins with an indirect arc followed by the downstroke which slightly retraces the end of it,

577

this is an AUTO GEAR SHIFT and the writer is an autocratic person who insists on having his own will, seeks to curb and limit others and does not easily allow them to speak their mind.

When in the cursive P (2), after the downstroke is made, the indirect arc slightly retraces the top, turns to the left, is drawn around or joins the tip of it, and ends by crossing or touching the downstroke near the top,

578

these are PARACHUTES and the writer is prone to protect his own interests first and to shift responsibility.

When the Foreign P (6) begins with the downstroke followed by a generous upcurve, which is drawn above and around it, crosses or joins the tip of it and ends in a small loop,

579

or when in the cursive P (2), after the downstroke is made, a generous curve begins at the right side, crosses it, is drawn above and around it and ends in a complete or incomplete loop above the starting point of the arc,

580

these are PALETTES and the writer shows uncanny skill at bluffing and tricking people.

When the printed P (4) starts with an indirect arc, which has a short upcurve, is longer at the left side of and forms an angle with a rather short downstroke,

581

this is a SICKLE and the writer is very discontented and has the urge to inflict injury.

When the downstroke of the cursive P (2) or printed P (4) ends in a hook or curve turned up, and when the indirect arc starts with a horizontal curve at the left side, is drawn above it and ends with a horizontal curve at the right side which may or may not join the downstroke,

582

these are RIDING CROPS ON A STAGE and the writer wants to be the focus of interest, exert influence on people, and control them.

When the cursive P (1) starts with a short downstroke followed by a retrace stroke and/or a long upstroke curving into the indirect arc, which is greater in height than in width or vice versa and may or may not join the downstroke,

583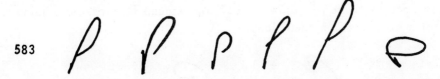

these are WHIPS HELD UP and the writer exercises authority to have mastery of people and situations.

When the downstroke of printed capitals as in the cursive P (2) narrows to a point,

584

or when in the printed p (8) the downstroke below the line narrows to a point,

585

these are STINGS OF A WASP and the writer is given to bickering, and provokes, criticizes, and belittles others.

When the cursive p (7) begins with the downstroke, and when the upstroke of the lower loop, which forms a narrow curve at the bottom and is long, crosses the downstroke near the top and ends in a point,

586

this is a LONG FISH and the writer is callous and ruthless.

When in the cursive p (7) the slightly concave or straight downstroke ends in a narrow curve or in a point below the line followed by the upstroke, which is straight or slightly convex, is at the right side of and close to the downstroke and is slightly retraced by a concavely curved, final stroke,

587

these are CENSURING FINGERS and the writer has the tendency to expose the imperfection of others and to reproach their shortcomings.

When the Foreign p (9) begins with a short, concave downstroke followed by a long, almost horizontal stroke which curves into the downstroke below the line,

588

this is a BROAD PROFILE OF NOSE and the writer has malicious joy in belittling others and their achievements.

When the cursive p (7) begins with the downstroke ending in a point below the line, and when a slightly convex upstroke, which ends in a small loop and joins the downstroke at the baseline, is at the right side of the downstroke,

589

this is a QUIVER and the writer is bitterly vindictive.

When in the cursive p (7) the lower loop is very large,

590

this is an INFLATED LOOP and the writer resorts to bluff to better be able to control people.

When in the cursive p (7) the straight initial upstroke forms an angle with the downstroke which ends in a point below the line, and when a straight upstroke, which is at the right side of and forms an angle with the downstroke, ends in a point, does not reach the baseline, and is parallel to the initial upstroke,

591

this is LIGHTNING and the writer because of quick adaptability and skill at sounding out others, can change his opinion and attitude so subtly that people do not notice his real intentions.

When in the Foreign p (9) the initial upstroke begins below the baseline and has almost the same length as the downstroke,

592

these are STILETTOS and the writer is hateful and can become violent.

When in the Foreign p (9) the part above the line, which has a loop, is bent forward more than the part below the line,

593

these are BODIES WITH HEAD BENT FORWARD and the writer by sub- servience and apparent devotion gives the impression of completely agree- ing with the ideas and wishes of others in order to better achieve his aims.

Chapter 30

LETTERS OF THE ALPHABET RESEMBLING PICTORIAL FORMS: LETTERS "Q" AND "q"

When the oval of the cursive q (6) begins with a convex upcurve which is made within the oval, and when the final upcurve touches the initial upcurve,

594

this is a DREAMY EYE and the writer knows how to evoke the good will of others and win their acceptance.

When the oval of the cursive q (6) is incomplete and the downstroke below the line, which ends in a point, is slightly retraced by a convex upstroke ending in a point above the line,

595

these are CENSURING FINGERS and the writer has the tendency to expose the imperfection of others and reproach their shortcomings.

Chapter 31

LETTERS OF THE ALPHABET RESEMBLING PICTORIAL FORMS: LETTERS "R" AND "r"

When the Foreign R (5) begins at the halfway mark with an oblong indirect arc which is parallel to slant of the following lower loop, and when the final downcurve which crosses the indirect arc or begins with a small loop, is slightly curved and extends below the baseline,

596

these are DRAGON FLIES and the writer can impress others as a kind and guileless person.

When the second part of the cursive R (2) stands alone, and when the indirect arc consists of a hook followed by a straight or convex downstroke which forms an angle with a short, horizontal stroke, and when the latter curves into a straight, final downstroke which ends in a point at the baseline,

597

this is a DEMONIAC PROFILE OF NOSE and the writer enjoys creating confusion and dissension, using schemes and plots so cunningly that no one holds him responsible.

When the second part of the cursive R (2) stands alone, and when the indirect arc begins at the left side of the preceding downstroke and is generously drawn above and around it, and when a vertical, almost straight, final downstroke slightly retraces the end of the arc,

598

this is an AUTO GEAR SHIFT and the writer is an autocratic person who insists on having his own will, seeks to curb and limit others, and does not easily allow them to speak their mind.

When in the Foreign R (6), after the first part is made, the indirect arc is parallel to slant and oblong, followed by a straight, final downstroke ending below the baseline,

599

this is a PARACHUTE and the writer is prone to protect his own interests first and to shift responsibility.

When the cursive R (1) begins with the downstroke followed by a generous curve which starts in the lower half and at the right side of the downstroke, crosses it, is generously drawn around it, and ends with a loop on it,

600

or when the Foreign R (6) starts with a short, convex downstroke followed by the indirect arc, which is generously drawn above and around it, and ends with a loop joining the tip of the initial downstroke,

601

these are PALETTES and the writer shows uncanny skill at bluffing and tricking others.

When the second part of the cursive R (1) stands alone, and when the indirect arc, the center loop and the long, straight, final stroke which ends far below the baseline, are in line,

602

or when in the cursive R (2) the indirect arc crosses the initial downstroke twice, and when a long, straight, final downstroke ends far below the baseline,

603

these are WRENCHES and the writer seeks to attain his aims by forcible means.

When the indirect arc of the cursive R (2), which is far greater in width than in height, begins with an extremely long horizontal stroke at the left side of and above the initial downstroke and ends at the tip of it,

604

this is a GIGANTIC WHIP TO THE RIGHT and the writer can curb others' freedom of action by harsh and drastic measures.

When in the Foreign R (5), which may or may not have a short, initial downstroke, the indirect arc is generously curved to the right, to the left, and ends in a narrow curve followed by the horizontal final stroke,

605

these are LAKES and the writer covers his questionable practices with a veneer of integrity and responsibility.

When in the cursive R (2) the indirect arc, which joins the down-stroke at the top only, forms an angle with a short, straight, almost horizontal stroke, and when the latter in turn forms an angle with a concave, horizontal curve which does not reach the baseline,

606

this is a PROFILE OF NOSE WITH PROTRUDING CHIN and the writer knows how to find the Achilles tendon in people and attack them in their vulnerable spots.

When the final downcurve of the cursive r (7) ends below the line and the final stroke is eliminated,

607

this is an ALGA and the writer gives the impression of agreement and cooperation but seeks to accomplish his purpose by underhanded practice.

When in the cursive r (8) a short, initial upstroke curves into the downstroke ending in a point and followed by a straight upstroke at the left side of the downstroke, which crosses and extends above the initial upstroke and has a tick-out stroke,

608

this is a BEAK OF A DUCK and the writer gives such a guileless and kindly impression that people do not suspect him of working against them.

When the cursive r (8) consists of a convex, left slanting downstroke which forms an angle with a long, concave, right slanting, almost horizontal, final stroke,

609

this is a BIRD WITH WINGS EXPANDED and the writer knows well how to show off and to emphasize his good traits in order to impress his world.

When in the cursive r (7), after the initial upstroke and a long left slanting tick are made, the slant line is concave and higher at the end, and when a concave, final downstroke, which is higher than the initial upstroke, retraces the end of the slant line, extends below the line and has no final stroke,

610

this is a FISH GASPING FOR AIR and the writer is shrewd and crafty in his way of taking advantage of people.

When the cursive r (7) begins with a long, horizontal, initial upstroke followed by a short, concave, left slanting downstroke and a long, horizontal, final stroke, and when the initial stroke is similar in form and dimension to the downstroke and the final stroke,

611

this is a SEA GULL and the writer devises secret and underhanded plans against the interest of those who trust him.

When in the cursive r (7) the initial upstroke directly curves into the concave, final downstroke followed by a short final stroke,

612

this is a DAZZLING SNAKE and the writer for reasons of self-protection employs many a clever stratagem.

When in the cursive r (7), after the upstroke is made, which may or may not end in an open or ink-filled loop, the slant line, which is either long or short, horizontal or downward slanting, decidedly curves into the final downstroke which may be long or short and/or generously concave followed by the final upstroke which is different in form, size and slant,

613

these are PROVOCATIVE BODIES and the writer applies his captivating and alluring charm to convey the impression of being ready to yield to the wishes of others but can reverse this attitude unexpectedly and wriggle out of a situation.

When in the cursive r (7) an almost straight upstroke is made followed by a tick and a short slant line, and when the final downstroke, which is almost parallel to the initial upstroke, curves into a straight, horizontal, final stroke,

614

this is a BODY WITH ARM RESTED and the writer maintains poise and self-control, even if it looks as if he had lost them.

When in the cursive r (7), after the upstroke is made, a long tick follows and a slant line which is short and concave, and when the final downstroke retraces the end of the slant line, and when the tick is almost parallel to slant of the top of the final downstroke,

615

these are GRASPING FINGERS and the writer very quickly takes advantage of any and every opportunity which will benefit him.

    When the downstroke of the cursive r (8) is pointed at the top, long, and forms an angle with a short, straight, left tending upstroke which in turn forms an angle with a long, convex, right tending upstroke crossing the downstroke in the lower half,

616

these are PLIERS and the writer tries to attain his aims by forcible means.

    When the initial upstroke of the cursive r (8) is straight and forms an angle with a left slanting downstroke which in turn forms an angle with a right slanting, straight final upstroke which is reduced at the top and has a tick-out stroke,

617

this is a CREVICE and the writer can disconcert, bewilder and confuse people to gain control over them.

    When in the cursive r (7), after the initial upstroke and the tick are made, a concave slant line and a final downstroke, which retraces the end of it, follow, and when the space between the upstroke and the downstroke widens towards the bottom,

618

these are CRATERS OF A VOLCANO and the writer is underhanded and has the urge to surreptitiously inflict injury.

    When in the cursive r (7) the straight initial upstroke forms an angle with a long slant line joining the straight final downstroke, and when the latter forms an angle with the slightly convex or straight, almost horizontal final stroke,

619

this is a SUBMARINE and the writer is so much concerned about safeguarding his own interests that he disregards those of others.

    When in the cursive r (7) a concave downstroke retraces the initial upstroke and curves into a short connecting line joining the succeeding cursive e (7), and when the latter is reduced at the top,

620

this is the NUMBER 6 and the writer craves money and possessions so intensely that he would do anything in his power to acquire them.

When the cursive r (8) begins with a short upcurve near the top, and when the downstroke ends in a right tending curve followed by the connecting line joining the top of the next loopless cursive f (7), and when the downstroke of the latter ends in a point and is slightly retraced by a straight connecting line joining the concave downstroke of the next cursive t (5) which in turn retraces the preceding connecting line, and when the bar, if any, does not cross the "t," and when a rather short connecting line joins the next cursive e (7) which may be higher than or at level with the preceding downstroke of the "t,"

621

this is the FRACTION 2/6 and the writer is very calculating and figures everything in dollars and cents before he takes any action.

When in the cursive r (8) the retrace upstroke forms an angle with a long connecting line joining the next cursive i (6), and when the space between the two letters widens towards the bottom,

622

these are SACRIFICIAL BLOCKS and the writer can be cruel and callous.

When in the cursive r (8) the initial upstroke begins at halfway mark, is straight, almost horizontal, and forms an angle with the downstroke, and when the retrace upstroke ends about halfway and forms an angle with a straight connecting line which is longer than the height of the preceding downstroke and joins the next i (6), and when the latter is reduced at the top,

623

these are COBBLE STONES and the writer is prone to vex and humiliate others by sarcastic and cynical remarks.

When the cursive r (8) begins with an upcurve near the top followed by the downstroke which is slightly retraced by a connecting line joining the next cursive o (5), and when the latter is reduced at the top, does not reach the baseline and is followed by an upward slanting connecting line joining the next cursive a (6), and when the latter is incomplete, higher than the preceding letters, and ends with a small loop which may or may not have a final stroke,

624

206

this is the NUMBER 206 and the writer may pretend that money is of little importance to him but in reality money means more to him than to the average person.

Chapter 32

LETTERS OF THE ALPHABET RESEMBLING PICTORIAL FORMS: LETTERS "S" AND "s"

When in the cursive S (1), after the horizontal curve at the baseline is made, a left tending indirect loop follows,

625

this is a LEFT TENDING ADDITIONAL LOOP and the writer cleverly hides malicious and perfidious designs.

When in the cursive S (1) at the lowest point of the downstroke a convex curve follows,

626

this is a REVERSED STROKE and the writer while enjoying the reputation as a man of fine character, would not hesitate to slander a person.

When the downstroke of the cursive S (1) extends far below the baseline and ends in a hook turned up to the right,

627

this is an ALGA and the writer gives the impression of agreement and cooperation but seeks to accomplish his purpose by underhanded practice.

When in the printed S (4, 4a) the upper curve consists of a slightly concave or straight initial downstroke which forms an angle with the lower curve,

628

these are PELICANS and the writer tends to point out the weaknesses of others and by carping criticism undermines their self-confidence.

179

When in the printed S (4, 4a) the upper and the lower part are differently shaped as to form and size,

629

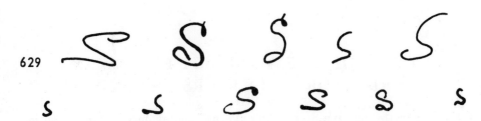

these are VIPERS and the writer can be so affable, kind and obliging that
everyone believes him friendly disposed and does not believe him capable
of falsehood and deceit.

When the cursive S (5) starts with the downcurve followed by an
upcurve which crosses the downcurve almost in the middle and joins the
starting point,

630

(this is the NUMBER 8)

or when the printed S (4, 4a) is crossed diagonally or when it is defective,

631

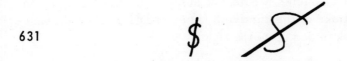

(these are IMPERFECT DOLLAR SIGNS)

these are NUMBERS AND SIGNS IN LETTERS and the writer craves money
and possessions so intensely that he would do everything to acquire them.

When in the cursive S (5), after the upstroke is made, the downstroke,
which may be straight, ends in a straight, horizontal or slightly upward
slanting stroke,

632

or when in the printed s (9) the initial downstroke ends in a straight horizontal stroke followed by a straight, right slanting upstroke which crosses
the downstroke and joins the starting point,

633

these are CHESS PAWNS and the writer has the tendency to vex, humiliate, and subdue people.

When the initial upstroke of the cursive S (5) begins above the baseline and forms a long loop with the downcurve, and when the final horizontal curve ends before it joins the initial upstroke and forms a shorter
loop by crossing the preceding downstroke in the lower half, and when
the final upstroke is almost parallel to the initial stroke,

634

or when the initial upstroke of the cursive s (8) begins above the baseline followed by the downstroke which begins and ends with a loop, and
when the loops have different slants and the lower one has a final upstroke which is almost parallel to the initial stroke,

635

these letters resemble the GERMAN SCRIPT h (9) and the writer can
exert influence on and take advantage of people.

When the cursive s (7, 8) begins with a hook down followed by a
concave, initial upstroke which curves into a convex downstroke, and
when the latter ends in a hook turned up to the left,

636

this is a HORSESHOE and the writer has the tendency to limit and restrict others and to force his will on them.

When the downstroke of the cursive s (7) is straight and ends in a
point before it reaches the baseline, and when the following concave curve
is horizontal and almost as long on the left as on the right side,

637

this is a SHOEMAKER'S HAMMER and the writer enjoys making people
feel small.

When in the cursive s (7) the downstroke is straight and ends in a
point followed by a straight or slightly concave, upward slanting stroke

which forms an angle with a long, concave, right tending, final stroke crossing the downstroke

638

these are PLIERS and the writer seeks to attain his goal by forcible means.

    When in the cursive s (7), after the upstroke is made, which may be straight, the straight downstroke forms an angle with a straight or slightly convex, left tending stroke joining the initial upstroke,

639

these are TRIANGLES IN SMALL LETTERS and the writer tends to point out the weaknesses of others and by carping criticism seeks to undermine their self-confidence.

    When the cursive s (7) begins with a long initial upstroke below the baseline followed by the downstroke and the horizontal curve crossing the initial upstroke,

640

this is a TURKISH SWORD and the writer can be callous and ruthless.

    When in the cursive s (8) at the end of the downstroke a loop is formed followed by a straight connecting line joining the top of the following cursive h (6), and when the latter is higher than the preceding letter and its downstroke slightly retraces the preceding connecting line,

641

these are BELLOWS and the writer is a show off and to reach his objective resorts to all sorts of tricks and ruses.

    When the initial upstroke of the cursive s (7) is almost straight and curves into the almost straight downstroke which ends in a point before it reaches the baseline, and when a straight, left tending, upward slanting stroke crosses the initial upstroke and is partly retraced by a slightly concave, right tending, horizontal connecting line which crosses the downstroke and joins the center of the next cursive o (5), which has no tick out stroke, is reduced at the top, and does not reach the baseline,

642

this is a CLAPPER OF A BELL and the writer is callous enough to resort to harsh and forcible means to control others.

LETTERS OF THE ALPHABET RESEMBLING PICTORIAL FORMS: LETTERS "T" AND "t"

. When the cursive T (2) begins with a concave, upward slanting, initial stroke followed by a short, decidedly convex downstroke ending in a left tending, concave, horizontal, final curve,

643

this is the HEAD OF A BIRD and the writer uses all sorts of maneuvers and schemes to intimidate people and make them accede to his will.

When the bar of the printed T (3) is above or generously drawn around the downstroke,

644

these are STAGES WITH A PERSON IN THE FRONT and the writer is eager to stand in the limelight and is longing for recognition and acknowledgment.

When the bar of the printed T (3), which consists of a long, convex curve, is above the downstroke and longer on the left side,

645

this is a STAGE WITH A PERSON ON THE SIDE and the writer wants to be the center of attraction but purposely places himself in the background to impress people as a modest and humble person.

When in the printed T (3) the downstroke slants to the right and at the lowest tip forms an angle with a straight, vertical upstroke which in turn forms an angle with the bar, and when the latter is about twice the height of the downstroke,

646

this is a HATCHET and the writer resorts to force and pressure to attain his goal.

When in the printed T (3) the bar which is heavily inked and heavier on one side is no more than half the height of the downstroke,

647

this is a HAMMER and the writer can be so callous that he can become ruthless.

When the initial upstroke of the cursive T (2) slants upwards, and when the downstroke, which is straight and ends in a point at the base-line, is at least twice the length of the upstroke,

648

this is a SCYTHE and the writer can be ruthless and unscrupulous.

When in the printed T (3) the bar, which slants upwards, is more than twice the height of the downstroke,

649

this is a PAIR OF SCALES and the writer wavers both in his ideas and in his actions.

When the downstroke of the printed T (3) ends in a curve turned up to the right or to the left, and when the bar, which may or may not join the downstroke, is longer than its height,

650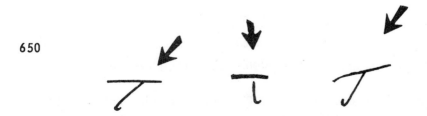

these are RIDING CROPS ON A PLANE and the writer wants to be the focus of interest, exert influence on people and control them.

When the downstroke of the printed T (3) is either slightly concave or convex at the end or is straight and ends in a curve turned up, and when the bar is concave,

651

these are RIDING CROPS ON A HILL and the writer by tyrannizing others can subtly create situations favorable for himself which place him in the limelight.

When the bar of the printed T (3) is slightly concave,

652

this is a HILL WITH A PERSON STANDING ON IT and the writer has an ardent desire to play an important role in life and be the center of attraction.

When the bar of the printed T (3) begins at the tip of the downstroke and joins the top of the printed h (7),

653

this is a PASSAGE WAY and the writer at times is prone to act illogically and do things without rhyme or reason.

When the bar of the printed T (3) is above the downstroke and forms an angle with the downstroke of the following printed h (7) which is not retraced by the rest of the letter,

654

this is an ANGLE IRON and the writer weighs all pros and cons before he takes any action.

When two consecutive printed TT (3) have one bar only which crosses both downstrokes near the top,

655

this is a BAMBOO GATE and the writer can unexpectedly and surreptitiously inflict injury.

When the initial stroke of the cursive T (2) is concave followed by a downstroke which is straight and ends in a point at the baseline,

656

or when in the printed T (3) the bar is generously concave, much longer than the height of the downstroke and longer to the left, and when the bar directly curves into the loop of the following cursive h (6) which is higher than the preceding letter,

657

these are ENTICING ARMS and the writer pretends kindness, congeniality, and obligingness so convincingly that others become unsuspecting and divulge plans which they otherwise would keep to themselves.

When in the printed T (3) the bar forms an angle with the right slanting downstroke which has almost the same length as the bar,

658

or when the cursive t (7) begins with a left slanting downstroke which forms an angle with the straight, final upstroke, and when the latter has almost the same length as the downstroke,

659

this is a WEDGE and the writer is liable to sow discord and foment strife.

When the bar of the printed T (3) is longer on one side of the downstroke and narrows to a point,

660

or when the bar of the cursive t (5), which may cross the downstroke near the top or join it, is longer on one side of the downstroke, and narrows to a point,

661

these are ICE AXES and the writer would not hesitate to use force and even pressure to make others pliable to his wishes.

When in the cursive T (1), after the indirect oval is made, a concave, upward slanting stroke follows which is partly retraced by the downstroke, and when the latter ends with a narrow concave curve followed by a stroke going back to the baseline,

662

or when the downstroke of the cursive t (5) has a small loop with the bar above it and ends in a point at the baseline, and when a straight connecting line joins the loop of the next cursive e (7) which may end with a downstroke below the loop, if any,

663

these are BELLOWS and the writer is a show off, and to reach his objective resorts to all sorts of tricks and ruses.

When the printed T (3) begins with a short, straight, initial upstroke followed by the downstroke, and when the bar begins with a short, straight, left tending stroke,

664

or when in the printed t (6) the downstroke ends in a hook turned up, and when the bar begins with a short, straight, left tending stroke,

665

or when the downstroke of the printed t (6) ends in a hook turned up, and when the bar ends with a hook turned down,

666

these are RIDING CROPS ONE UPON THE OTHER and the writer enjoys harassing and tormenting others and showing them that he has them in his power.

When the cursive T (1) begins with a slightly convex or straight upstroke at the baseline followed by a straight downstroke, which partly retraces it, and ends in a point,

667

or when in the cursive t (7), after the upstroke is made, a downstroke follows, which does not reach the baseline, and forms an angle with a straight, horizontal, final stroke,

668

these are DAGGER BLADES and the writer by using pressure and intimidation tries to force people into his services.

When the bar of the printed T (3) or cursive t (5) is above the downstroke and has hooks or curves turned down on both ends,

669

these are BRACKETS and the writer would not hesitate to use forceful means to control others.

When the cursive "t" or to (5) ends with a convex, left tending upcurve joining or crossing the downstroke of the "t" and forming a horizontal loop with the bar which is much longer to the left,

670

these are TRAINERS' WHIPS and the writer strives to control situations by pestering, harassing and vexing others so that they are unable to offer resistance.

When in the cursive t (5) at the lowest point of the long, straight downstroke, a straight, left tending upstroke joins the bar which is concave,

671

these are PLIERS and the writer seeks to attain his goal by forcible means.

When the downstroke of the cursive t (5) ends in a point followed by a straight or convex, left tending upstroke which forms an angle with or is slightly retraced by the bar, and when the latter, which is longer than the downstroke and may be concave, is longer on the right side,

672

these are FOLDING CHAIRS and the writer can trick, trap, and outwit people.

When in the cursive t (5) at the lowest tip of the straight downstroke a straight left tending upstroke follows which forms an angle with a long, downward slanting bar,

673

this is a SMALL HATCHET and the writer when his feelings are hurt, will seek revenge.

When in the cursive t (5) the bar consists of a double curve which joins the tip of the downstroke,

674

or when the cursive t (5) has a loop, the bar is slightly concave and crosses the loop near the top,

675

or when the bar of the printed t (6) is generously concave and crosses the downstroke near the top,

676

these are HORNS and the writer can become very obstinate and stubborn and will insist upon carrying out his ideas regardless of opposition and consequence.

    When the cursive t (5) has a loop and the bar is slightly concave, slants downward, and crosses the loop near the top,

677

these are BULL'S HORNS and the writer would not hesitate to use any means in his power to revenge himself on anyone who has offended him.

    When in the cursive t (5), after the initial upstroke is made, a short downstroke, which does not reach the baseline, partly retraces it, and when the final stroke, which is almost horizontal, is similar in form and dimension to the initial upstroke, and when the bar, if any, does not cross the downstroke,

678

this is a SEA GULL and the writer devises secret and underhanded plans against the interest of those who trust him.

    When in the cursive t (5) a straight or almost straight upstroke begins high above the baseline and forms a loop with the straight or almost straight downstroke ending in a point at the baseline, and when the bar, if any, is above the downstroke,

679

this is a SHEAF OF GRAIN and the writer has an uncanny ability to adapt himself to people, to speak their language, and to integrate himself so artfully with them that they believe he is on their side.

When in the printed t (6) the downstroke below the bar is eliminated,

680

these are TRUNKS OF A TREE and when the writer loses interest in people, he will be icy, haughty, and pretend that he does not know them.

When the downstroke of the cursive t (5) or printed t (6) narrows to a point,

681

these are STINGS OF A WASP and the writer is given to bickering, and provokes, criticizes, and belittles others.

When the downstroke of the cursive t (5) is partly round or pointed at the baseline, and when the final upstroke is concave,

682

these are PROFILES OF HOOKED NOSES and the writer can be friendly to one's face but at the same time harbor malicious and wicked designs.

When in the cursive t (5) the initial upstroke is almost horizontal followed by a short, vertical downstroke, which partly retraces the preceding stroke, and has an almost horizontal final stroke, and when the latter has about the same length as the initial stroke, and when the bar is short and crosses low,

683

or when in the cursive t (5) the initial upstroke, which begins with a concave, horizontal curve, is slightly retraced by a straight, left slanting downstroke, and when the latter ends in a point at the baseline and the bar, which joins the downstroke, is long and longer to the left,

684

these are CHINESE ORNAMENTS and the writer is very subtle in pretending feelings of loyalty and friendship so that no one would ever suspect him of being unfaithful and disloyal.

When the bar of the printed t (6) or cursive t (5) which is much longer on the right side, extends over the whole word and does not touch or cross any following tall letter or letters,

685

these are ROOMS WITHOUT RIGHT WALL and the writer can present himself in a favorable light and win the confidence of people but their trust in him is not always justified.

When the bar of the printed t (6) or cursive t (5), which is much longer on the left side, extends over the whole word and does not cross or touch any preceding tall letter or letters,

686

these are ROOMS WITHOUT LEFT WALL and the writer has wicked intentions.

When the bar of the cursive t (5) extends over the whole word and crosses another loopless "t" or tall letter near or joins it at the top,

687

these are HIGH STAGES and the writer is a showman and knows how to put on an act successfully in order to impress his world.

When the downstrokes of the cursive t (5) are very short, and when the bar is very long and joins and/or crosses another "t",

688

or when the cursive t's (5) have loops and the bar, which crosses the downstroke below the loop, crosses another "t" below the loop,

688a

these are LOW STAGES and the writer wants to play first fiddle and achieve recognition.

When in the cursive t (5) or in the printed t (6) the downstroke and the bar are evenly inked, and when the bar, which is one-half to two-thirds of the height of the downstroke, crosses the latter about one-third from the top,

689

these are RELIGIOUS CROSSES and the writer is ready to extend himself for others and performs unselfish acts.

When the bar of the printed t (6) or cursive t (5) is about one-third from the top of the downstroke but in proportion to is either too short,

690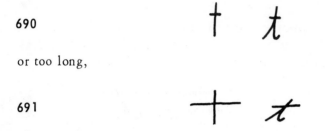

or too long,

691

or one side is longer,

692

or the downstroke is curved,

693

or the bar is slanted,

694

or the bar is heavier or lighter inked than the downstroke,

695

these are FALSE RELIGIOUS CROSSES and the writer pretends to cherish ideals and people are inclined to consider him unselfish and interested in their well-being.

When in the cursive t (5) or printed t (6) the downstroke and the bar have almost the same length and are evenly inked, and when the bar crosses the downstroke about one-fourth from the top,

696

these are PROTECTIVE GESTURES and the writer is fair and does not judge people before all evidence is in.

When in the cursive t (5) or printed t (6) the bar is about one-fourth from the top of the downstroke but in proportion to it and is either too long,

697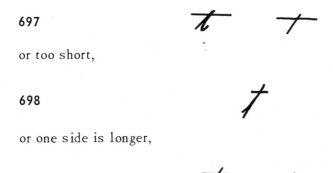

or too short,

698

or one side is longer,

699

or the bar is heavier or lighter inked than the downstroke,

700

or the downstroke is curved,

701

these are DECEPTIVE GESTURES and the writer pretends to be helpful, kind, and righteous but in reality is selfish, unkind, and unrighteous.

When the downstroke of the cursive t (5), which is straight and ends in a point at the baseline, or the downstroke of the printed t (6) slants to the left, and when the bars, which are one-half to two-thirds of the height of the downstrokes, cross the latter about one-third from the top and are at right angles with the downstrokes,

702

these are TOTTERING CROSSES and the writer shows little respect for others, their actions, and achievements.

When a word begins with a cursive t (5), which has no initial stroke, and ends with another cursive t (5) which has no final stroke, and when there are only small letters between the two t's, and when the bar begins at the top of the first "t," joins the second one and extends to the right far beyond the word,

703

this is a BANNER and the writer tries to hide his emotions by maintaining an outwardly cheerful attitude.

When in the cursive t (7) at the lowest point of the downstroke a convex, left tending upstroke follows which ends in a short curve turned down,

704

this is a BARBED HOOK and the writer does not easily forget a wrong and will call to account anyone who dares to offend him.

When in the cursive t (5) a short, concave bar begins on the downstroke and extends to the right,

705

these are MEAT HOOKS and the writer can be hard and ruthless on his opponents.

When in the cursive t (5) the bar is very short, slants downward, narrows to a point and is either above the downstroke, crosses it near the top or touches it,

706

these are NAILS and the writer is callous and ruthless and will compel people to comply with his wishes.

When the bar of the printed t (6) starts almost in the center of and on the downstroke, extends to the right, and is about twice the height of the downstroke,

707

this is a RAKE and the writer is of a domineering nature.

When the downstroke of the cursive t (5) is straight, ends in a point and is slightly retraced by the short, concave, connecting line curving

into the convex downstroke of the next cursive s (8) which ends in a
point below the baseline,

708

this is a DEVIL'S FORK and the writer under the mask of kindness and
service can cause all kinds of difficulties and confusion.

When the cursive t (5), which has no final stroke, and the printed
t (6) have bars, which are longer to the right and either begin on the downstroke or cross it slightly, and when the bars may or may not end in a
short hook or curve turned down, parallel to the preceding downstroke,

709

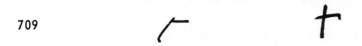

these are GALLOWS TO THE RIGHT and the writer enjoys exposing
people and making them objects to ridicule.

When the cursive t (5), which has no final stroke, and the printed t
(6) have bars which are longer to the left and either begin on the downstroke or cross it slightly, and when the bars may or may not end in a
short hook or curve turned down, parallel to the preceding downstroke,

710

these are GALLOWS TO THE LEFT and the writer is liable to bear a
deep grudge and waits for an opportunity to retaliate.

When the long bar of the cursive t (5) begins with a hook or curve
turned up and either joins the tip of the downstroke or is above it,

711

these are RIDING CROPS HELD TO THE LEFT and the writer has the
tendency to force his will on others so cleverly that they are not aware of
his dictatorial intentions.

When the bar of the printed t (6) or cursive t (5) is extremely long,
ends in a hook or curve turned down and is above the downstroke or begins
on it,

712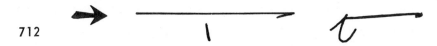

these are RIDING CROPS HELD TO THE RIGHT and the writer has the tendency to control people and situations and can become very authoritative if people do not comply with his wishes.

When the bar of the cursive t (5), which is extremely long, starts with a hook or curve turned up or down and crosses the following tall letters,

713

these are RIDING CROPS ON TWO STEMS and the writer's domineering tendencies are so powerful that he can seriously interfere with the plans of others.

When in the cursive to (5) the upstroke of the oval extends beyond the downstroke, curves to the left and crosses the preceding strokes, or when in the cursive t (5) at the lowest point of the downstroke a left tending, convex upstroke follows, and when the upstrokes form angles with or are slightly retraced by or curve into long bars,

714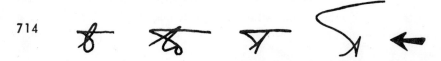

these are TRAINERS' WHIPS and the writer strives to control situations by pestering, harassing, and vexing others so that they are unable to offer resistance.

When the bar of the printed t (6) or cursive t (5) is in the lower half and at the right side of the downstroke and does not touch it,

715

these BARS RESEMBLE DASHES and the writer can be so aloof, icy, and reserved that others are kept at a distance.

When the cursive t (7) begins with the downstroke followed by a long, final upstroke,

716

this is an INSERT and the writer always finds something to object, to criticize, and to reproach.

When the cursive t (5) begins with a decidedly convex upstroke forming a long loop with the downstroke, and when the latter ends near the
starting point of the initial stroke and a short bar, if any, crosses the downstroke,

717

this is a MELANCHOLY MOON and the writer has times of indifference
and lack of interest when he is cool, icy and reserved.

When the initial upstroke of the cursive t (7) is decidedly concave,
begins above the baseline and forms an angle with the downstroke which
joins the starting point of the preceding upstroke, and when the bar, if
ary, is above the downstroke,

718

this is a MOON ON THE WANE IN UPPER LOOPS and the writer at times
can be affable and friendly, at others, cool, icy and reserved.

When in the cursive t (5) the bar, which may be shorter or longer
than the downstroke, crosses it almost in the middle, and when the two
sides of the bar have almost the same length,

719

or when in the cursive th (5, 6) the bar, which may be shorter or longer
than the downstroke, does not cross the short "t" and crosses the downstroke of the following loopless "h" almost in the middle, and when the
two sides of the bar have almost the same length,

720

these are IMPERFECT PLUS SIGNS and the writer's main concern is to
gain profit for himself.

When the downstroke of the cursive t (5), which is very short, curves
to the left on the baseline and the end of the curve joins the bar which
is concave and crosses the downstroke almost in the middle,

721

these are ROW BOATS and the writer dislikes committing himself and
wriggles out of situations which impose too much responsibility on him.

When the downstroke of the cursive t (5) or the downstroke of the printed t (6) is decidedly concave, and the final stroke is eliminated or almost eliminated, and when the bar, which slightly crosses the downstroke or touches it almost in the center, is longer on the right,

722

or when the cursive t (5) has a loop which is pointed or partly round, and when the bar which crosses the loop or crosses one side and touches the other, is longer on one side,

723
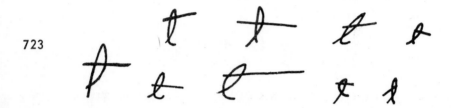

these are BOWS AND ARROWS and the writer can be friendly to a person's face but is liable to inflict injury surreptitiously.

When in the cursive t (5) the downstroke, which is very short and ends in a point, forms an angle with a short, slightly concave, wide, left tending upstroke which curves into the bar, and when the latter crosses the downstroke in the middle,

724

this is a BROKEN SABER and the writer weakens in his endeavor to fight for a cause and in spite of the best intentions he can be induced to alter his course.

When the downstroke of the cursive t (5) ends in a point and forms an angle with a short, wide, slightly concave, left tending upstroke which curves into the bar, and when the latter, which crosses the downstroke in the lower half, is much longer at the right,

725

this is a CAVALRY SABER and the writer is ready to employ force to make others yield to his wishes.

When in the printed t (6), after a long downstroke is made, a very short bar crosses it near the baseline,

726

this is a FENCING FOIL LIFTED and the writer can become very stubborn and obstinate.

When the downstroke of the printed t (6) is short, and when the bar, which crosses the downstroke almost in the middle, is at least three times the height of it, much longer at the right, and narrows to a point,

727

this is a FENCING FOIL ON GROUND and the writer has the tendency to annoy, needle, and offend others.

When in the printed t (6), after the downstroke is made, a generously concave, horizontal bar crosses it in the lower half,

728

this is an ANTIQUE SWORD LIFTED and the writer wants to attract the attention of his world by pretending to be idealistically inclined and ready to extend himself for others.

When in the printed t (6), after the downstroke is made, a convex bar crosses it in the upper half,

729

this is an ANTIQUE SWORD LOWERED and the writer will not make any direct attack but will resort to schemes and plots.

When the downstroke of the printed t (6) has a double curve followed by a short bar,

730

or when in the cursive t (5) the downstroke slants far to the right and ends in a point at the baseline, and when the bar consists of a long, almost vertical, double curve which begins above and ends below the downstroke,

731

these are TURKISH SWORDS and the writer can be callous and ruthless in pursuing his aims.

When in the cursive te (5, 7) the downstroke of the "t" slants to the left followed by a horizontal connecting line joining the "e," and when the downstroke below the loop is eliminated and the concave, horizontal final stroke is similar in form and size to the downstroke of the "t" and the following connecting line,

732

or when in the cursive th (5, 6) the downstroke of the "t" is very short and concave followed by a horizontal connecting line joining the stubby loop of the "h," and when the downstroke below the loop, which is almost eliminated, curves into a concave, almost horizontal stroke, and when the latter is similar in form and size to the downstroke of the "t" and the following connecting line,

733

these are SPIDERS and the writer is very smart in handling people, can win them by charm and affability, and like a spider can get them into his web.

When the cursive t (5) begins with a concave downstroke followed by a short connecting line which joins the succeeding cursive e (7), and when the bar, if any, does not cross the downstroke,

734

this is the NUMBER 6 and the writer craves money and possessions so intensely that he would do anything in his power to acquire them.

When in the printed T (3), after the downstroke is made, a concave bar directly curves into the short loop of the next cursive h (7) which is higher than the preceding letter,

735

these are CHINESE DOORS and the writer is anxious to hide his real thoughts, feelings, and intentions.

When the cursive t (5) begins with a short downstroke ending in a point, and when a retrace upstroke extends above it and curves into the loopless downstroke of the next cursive h (6) which is higher than the preceding letter,

736

these are DOORWAYS and the writer has the tendency to exaggerate and dramatize to better gain his ends.

When the bar of the cursive t (5) is above the downstroke, narrows to a point, and crosses the concave back of the loop of the next cursive h (6),

737

this is a MOON WITH ROCKET and the writer can be friendly one moment, cutting and mean the next.

When in the cursive t (5), after the downstroke is made, a long, almost horizontal connecting line joins the downstroke of the next cursive s (8) or i (6) which end in a point below the line and slant to the left,

738

these are PROFILES OF BROAD NOSES and the writer has malicious joy in belittling others and their achievements.

When in the cursive t (5) the downstroke begins with a short hook or curve, and when a horizontal connecting line curves into the next cursive i (6) which is short, slants to the left, and ends in a point, or when an almost straight, slightly upward slanting connecting line joins the next cursive o (5) which does not reach the baseline,

739

these are DEMONIAC PROFILES OF NOSES and the writer enjoys creating confusion and dissension, using schemes and plots so cunningly that no one holds him responsible.

When in the cursive t (5) a straight downstroke curves into a convex, almost horizontal connecting line which in turn curves into the short, left slanting, succeeding cursive i (6) ending in a point below the baseline, or when the connecting line curves into the short, convex downstroke of the next cursive s (8) ending below the baseline, or when the connecting line curves into the deflated, left slanting, indirect oval of the next cursive o (5) ending below the baseline,

740

these are PROFILES OF NOSES WITH WIDE NOSTRILS and the writer has malicious joy in surreptitiously inflicting injury.

    When the printed t (6) consists of a downstroke only which is retraced halfway, and when a convex, horizontal, connecting line curves into the indirect oval of the next cursive o (5) which ends abruptly at the baseline, and when a convex upcurve slightly retraces the end of the preceding curve and joins the connecting line,

741

this is a DULL BEAK and the writer is callous and ruthless in pursuing his aims.

    When in the cursive t (5) the downstroke, which does not reach the baseline, retraces the upstroke, and when a short connecting line joins the next cursive o (5) which partly retraces the connecting line, slants in a different direction than the preceding letter, and has no tick out stroke,

742

these are LAMPS WITH A GOOSE NECK and the writer feigns warm feelings for others so that they believe him ready to sacrifice.

    When the cursive t (5) begins with the downstroke followed by a short, horizontal connecting line which joins the next cursive o (5), and when the latter is half above and half below the baseline and has no tick-out stroke,

743

this is a PISTON and the writer can enforce his will and command respect.

    When the cursive t (5) begins with the downstroke followed by a short connecting line joining the indirect oval of the next cursive o (5) which is half above and half below the baseline and has no tick-out stroke, and when the bar is very long and longer to the right,

744

or when in the printed t (6), after the downstroke and the bar are made, the latter curves into the indirect oval of the next printed o (6) which does not reach the baseline,

745

these are LANTERNS and the writer is inclined to pose and show off in order to impress his world.

When in the printed t (6) the bar forms an angle with the next incomplete, printed o (6) which has a longer upcurve and does not reach the baseline,

746

this is an INSTRUMENT OF TORTURE and the writer can harass people until they submit to his wishes.

When in the printed t (6), after the downstroke is made, the bar, if any, stands alone, and when two printed o's (6) follow, which are gradually higher, do not reach the baseline, and are reduced at the top,

747

this is the NUMBER 100 and the writer pretends that money is of little importance to him but in reality money means more to him than to the average person.

When the cursive t (5) consists of a downstroke only, and when the connecting line curves into the downstroke of the next cursive r (8) ending in a point,

748

this is a GROVELING SNAKE and the writer can be friendly towards a person one day and betray him the next.

When the first downstroke of two consecutive cursive t's (5) does not reach the baseline and is higher than the downstroke of the second "t" which ends in a point or in a short curve below the baseline, and when the bar crosses both downstrokes or touches one downstroke and crosses the other,

749

these are PIERCED FINGERS and the writer makes promises but always
with mental reservations.

Chapter 34

LETTERS OF THE ALPHABET RESEMBLING PICTORIAL FORMS: LETTERS ''U'' AND ''u''

When in the cursive U (1), after the indirect initial loop or the short upcurve is made, the first downcurve follows, and when the intermediate stroke is either concave, has a double curve, or is convex,

750

these are VIPERS and the writer can be so affable, kind, and obliging that everyone believes him friendly disposed and does not believe him capable of falsehood and deceit.

When the printed u (8) narrows at the top,

751

these are HORSESHOES and the writer has the tendency to limit and restrict others and to force his will on them.

When in the cursive u (6) the intermediate stroke curves into the second downstroke, which is reduced at the top, slants to the left, and does not reach the baseline, and when a short connecting line joins the succeeding cursive l (6) which slants to the right,

752

these letters resemble the GREEK THETA t (8) and the writer is a perfect showman, can talk of matters of which he has but little knowledge so convincingly that people are impressed and believe him to be an expert in the particular field or subject.

When in the cursive our (5, 6, 7) the intermediate stroke and the second downstroke of the ''u,'' which slants to the left, the connecting line and the downstroke of the next ''r,'' which is concave and slants to the left, are higher than the first downstroke of the ''u,''

753   *oᴄɹ*

this is a GLACIER and the writer is clever at shifting responsibility and letting others take the blame.

When in the cursive u (6) the second downstroke slants to the left, and when a connecting line joins the next looped cursive t (5) which slants to the right and has a final upstroke,

754   *ut*

this is an UNUSUAL ANCHOR and the writer feels insecure, is irresolute, vacillating in his opinion, not steadfast in purpose and will frequently change his course of action.

Chapter 35

LETTERS OF THE ALPHABET RESEMBLING PICTORIAL FORMS: LETTERS "V" AND "v"

When the cursive V (1) begins at halfway mark with a large incomplete loop followed by the downstroke and a convex, final upstroke,

755

or when the cursive V (1) begins with a short or long, concave, upward or downward slanting stroke followed by the downstroke and a convex, final upstroke,

756

these are VIPERS and the writer can be so affable, kind, and obliging that everyone believes him friendly disposed and does not believe him capable of falsehood and deceit.

When the cursive V (1) begins with a short, straight, initial upstroke which is slightly retraced by a straight downstroke, and when the latter is slightly retraced by a straight or slightly convex upstroke forming an angle with a long, straight, horizontal final stroke which is almost at level with the preceding downstroke,

757

these are SQUARE ROOTS and the writer is very self-centered and does nothing without hoping to benefit.

When the cursive V (2) or v (6) narrows at the top and has no tick-out stroke,

758

these are HORSESHOES and the writer has the tendency to limit and re-strict others and to force his will on them.

When the straight, horizontal, initial upstroke of the cursive v (5) curves into the downcurve, and when the upcurve is longer than the pre-ceding curve and not parallel to it,

759

these are CREVICES and the writer can disconcert, bewilder and con-fuse people to gain control over them.

When the final upcurve of the cursive v (5) forms an angle with a long connecting line joining the succeeding cursive i (6), and when the space between the two letters widens towards the bottom,

760

this is a SACRIFICIAL BLOCK and the writer is cruel and callous.

When the downcurve of the cursive v (5) partly retraces the initial upstroke, and when the final upcurve forms an angle with a short, straight, connecting line which joins the following cursive i (6), and when the latter does not reach the baseline,

761

this is the NUMBER 5 LYING ON THE LINE and the writer tries to impress people by pretending to be highly interested in their well-being and to be ready to extend himself for them.

When in the printed V (3) or v (7), after the first downstroke is made, an upstroke follows which is longer than the downstroke and may be con-cave,

762

these are INSERTS and the writer always finds something to object to, to criticize and to reproach.

When in the printed v (7) the space between the two downstrokes is much greater than their height,

763

this is a SEA GULL and the writer devises secret and underhanded plans against the interest of those who trust him.

LETTERS OF THE ALPHABET RESEMBLING PICTORIAL FORMS: LETTERS "W" AND "w"

When the cursive W (1) begins with the downstroke followed by a shorter intermediate stroke which retraces it to a great extent and curves into the second downstroke, and when the latter, which is shorter than the first one, is retraced by a long final upstroke,

764

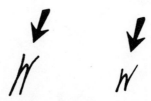

these are GRASPING FINGERS and the writer very quickly takes advantage of any and every opportunity which will benefit him.

When the Foreign W (4) begins with a convex downstroke ending in a point followed by a short, concave intermediate stroke curving into a short second downstroke which ends below the baseline and curves into the final upstroke,

765

this is a PROFILE OF PUG NOSE and the writer is prone to vex and humiliate others by sarcastic and cynical remarks.

When the center strokes of the printed W (3) cross in the upper half,

766

this is a HERALDIC SYMBOL and the writer tries to impress his world as trustworthy and reliable by pretending to be punctillious about conventions.

When the center part of the printed W (3) is greatly reduced at the top,

767

this is a CROWN and the writer pretends to acknowledge the superiority of others but actually wants to have the reins in his own hands and tries to attain his goal by employing many a clever stratagem or effectual force.

When the center part of the cursive W (2) has a vertical loop, and when the upstroke of the loop slants into the pointed top which is slightly retraced by the concave back of the loop, and when the crossing of the loop is very low and the downstroke below it turns to the right at the point where the crossing ends,

768

this is a CANDLE WITH STEADY FLAME and the writer feigns warm feelings for others so that they believe him ready to extend himself for them.

When in the cursive W (1) the second part stands alone and consists of a downstroke and a final upstroke which may be longer than or have the same length as the preceding downstroke,

769

this is an INSERT and the writer always finds something to object to, to criticize, and to reproach.

When in the cursive W (1), after the second downstroke is made, a straight or convex final upstroke, which has at least the same length as the preceding downstroke, forms an angle with a long, straight, horizontal stroke,

770

these are SQUARE ROOTS and the writer is very self-centered and does nothing without hoping to benefit.

When the cursive W (2) begins with a straight or slightly concave initial upstroke at the baseline followed by the first downstroke which is much longer than the rest of the letter,

771

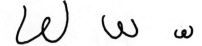

this is a TOWER and the writer can harass, embarrass, and infuriate people so that they lose their self-confidence enabling him to impose his will.

When the initial and the final stroke of the cursive W (2) or w (6) are decidedly curved, the tick-out stroke is eliminated, and the center part, which has a loop, is reduced at the top,

772

these are SPIDERS and the writer is very smart in handling people, can win them by charm and affability, and like a spider can get them into his web.

When in the cursive W (1) or w (5), after a straight downstroke is made, a much shorter, straight, intermediate stroke follows, and when a second downstroke, which is reduced at the top and does not reach the baseline, partly retraces the intermediate stroke or forms an angle with it, and when a straight or convex final upstroke follows,

773

these are POINTED FINGERS and the writer would not hesitate to coerce people into submission.

When in the cursive W (2) or w (6), after the first downstroke is made, a shorter intermediate stroke follows, and when a second downstroke, which is reduced at the top and does not reach the baseline, partly retraces the intermediate stroke and has a final upstroke,

774

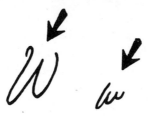

these are AUTHORITATIVE FINGERS and the writer has the tendency to browbeat and humiliate others.

When the center part of the cursive w (6) is reduced at the top, and when the first part of the letter is shaped differently than the second one,

775

these are DEFORMED BUTTOCKS and the writer wants to make life easy for himself, dislikes making any effort, and never volunteers to do anything.

When the final upcurve of the cursive w (5, 6), which has no tick-out stroke, curves into the following cursive b (6) or l (6) which have short pointed loops and long downstrokes below the loop,

776

these are SHEARS and the writer is cruel and his machinations are at times harmful.

When the final upcurve of the cursive w (5, 6), which has no tick-out stroke, decidedly curves to the left, and when a straight, horizontal, connecting line slightly retraces the end of the preceding upcurve and joins the tip of the succeeding cursive i (6) which does not reach the baseline,

777

these are an ANVIL and the writer resorts to ruthless and forcible means to gain his ends.

When the final upcurve of the cursive w (5) forms an angle with a long, connecting line joining the succeeding cursive i (6), and when the space between the two letters widens towards the bottom,

778

this is a SACRIFICIAL BLOCK and the writer is cruel and callous.

When in the cursive w (5, 6) the final upstroke, which has no tick-out stroke, forms an angle with a short, straight, connecting line joining the succeeding cursive i (6), which has a short final stroke, if any, or the "o (5)" which is incomplete and has no tick-out stroke, and when the two letters "i" and "o" do not reach the baseline,

779

these are NUMBERS 5 LYING ON THE LINE and the writer seeks to impress people by pretending to be highly interested in their well-being and to be ready to extend himself for them.

When the final upstroke of the cursive w (5) is longer than the preceding downstroke and has no tick-out stroke, and when a straight, downward slanting, connecting line joins the next cursive i (6), which is reduced at the top, slopes to the left, has a short final stroke, if any, and does not reach the baseline,

780

this is a TORPEDO BOAT and the writer is prone to complain, nag, and find fault with others.

LETTERS OF THE ALPHABET RESEMBLING PICTORIAL FORMS: LETTERS "X" AND "x"

When the printed X (3) begins at the top with a right slanting down-stroke followed by a right slanting upstroke which slightly retraces it, and when a vertical, final downstroke slightly retraces the preceding upstroke and crosses the initial downstroke,

781

this is a FOLDING TABLE and the writer is interested in a person only as long as he has something to offer him.

When the second part of the cursive X (1) stands alone and is higher than the first one,

782

this is the NUMBER 6 and the writer craves money and possessions so intensely that he would do anything in his power to acquire them.

When the left slanting stroke of the printed X (3) is decidedly convex, and when the right slanting stroke is much longer below the crossing,

783

this is a BOW AND ARROW and the writer can be friendly to a person's face but is liable to inflict injury surreptitiously.

When in the cursive x (6) the first downstroke is pointed at the top and forms a concave horizontal curve, which does not reach the baseline, and when the final downstroke, which begins and ends in a point, crosses the preceding curve almost in the center,

784

this is the NUMBER 4 and the writer craves money and possessions so intensely that he would do anything in his power to acquire them.

When in the cursive x (6) the space between the downstrokes is wide, and when a straight horizontal stroke begins on the first downstroke and joins or slightly crosses the second one, which has no final down-stroke, almost in the center,

785

this is a HORN and the writer can become very obstinate and stubborn and will insist on carrying out his ideas regardless of opposition and conse-quences.

LETTERS OF THE ALPHABET RESEMBLING PICTORIAL FORMS: LETTERS "Y" AND "y"

When the upper part of the printed Y (3) consists of a decidedly concave, narrow, horizontal curve which does not join the downstroke,

786

this is a TOPPLING HORN and the writer is prone to act illogically and do things without rhyme or reason.

When the first downstroke of the printed Y (3) is slightly concave or has a double curve, and when one of the two downstrokes or both begin with a hook or curve, and when the usual second and third strokes are made in one,

787

these are HAY FORKS and the writer resorts to force and pressure to achieve his goal.

When the printed Y (3) simply consists of two downstrokes, which stand alone, and is followed by the letter "o,"

788

or when the printed Y (3) consists of a short, straight downstroke which forms an angle with a short, straight upstroke ending on the final downstroke which is higher and followed by the letter "o" which stands alone,

789

these are the FRACTIONS 1/0 and the writer is very calculating and designing and figures everything in dollars and cents before he takes any action.

When the cursive Y (1) begins with the downcurve followed by a much shorter upcurve,

790

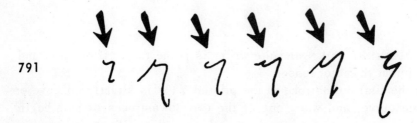

or when in the cursive y (5) the initial downstroke is pointed at the top followed by a horizontal or upward slanting, concave stroke which either curves into or forms an angle with a straight or concave final downstroke, and when the latter ends in a hook or curve turned up to the right below the line,

791

or when in the cursive y (5) the part above the line consists of an almost horizontal stroke which curves into a concave, final downstroke below the line, and when the latter ends in a hook or curve turned up to the right,

792

these are DEMONIAC PROFILES OF NOSES and the writer enjoys creating confusion and dissension, using schemes and plots so cunningly that no one holds him responsible.

When the second downstroke of the cursive y (5) above the line is shorter than the first or is almost eliminated, and when the first downstroke is pointed at the top and round or pointed at the bottom, and when the intermediate stroke curves into the straight, loopless final stroke below the line,

793

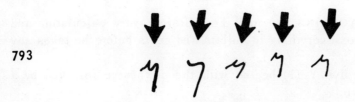

these are SMOOTH PROFILES OF NOSES and the writer is two-faced, apparently friendly but at the same time scheming how best to condition others in order to take advantage of them.

When in the cursive y (5) the second upstroke above the line forms an angle with a convex, final downstroke, and when the upstroke of the lower loop crosses the downstroke near the top or ends on it and retraces it to the end,

794

these are CLUBS HELD DOWN and the writer is hot-tempered and inclined to vent his rage on others.

When in the cursive y (5) at the lowest point of the final downstroke a left tending, downward or upward slanting, convex stroke follows which may or may not retrace the downstroke slightly, and when a right tending, straight, final stroke which may or may not cross the final downstroke, slightly retraces the preceding upcurve,

795

these are WEBBED FEET and the writer can hide his selfish intentions so cleverly that people who later notice that they have been taken advantage of, are quite surprised that he is capable of such an act.

When in the cursive y (5, 6) the downstroke below the line curves into, forms an angle with or is slightly retraced by a convex, left tending, horizontal or slightly upward slanting stroke,

796

these are REVERSED STROKES BELOW THE LINE and the writer can be maliciously and wickedly underhanded.

When in the cursive y (5, 6) the downstroke below the line is slightly retraced by or curves into a convex, left tending, horizontal or upward slanting stroke which forms an indirect loop with the following final upstroke,

797

these are LEFT TENDING ADDITIONAL LOOPS BELOW THE LINE and the writer is vengefully malevolent.

When in the cursive y (5) the initial upstroke is straight and forms an angle with the following center curve which is higher at the end, and when the convex final downstroke slightly retraces the end of the preceding curve and ends in a left tending, concave, horizontal curve below the line,

798

this is a HEAD OF A BIRD and the writer uses all sorts of maneuvers and schemes to intimidate people and make them accede to his will.

When in the cursive y (5) the part above the line consists of an almost straight, initial upstroke which is slightly retraced by a concave, left and downward slanting, center curve and ends in a point below the line,

799

this is a FISH GASPING FOR AIR and the writer is shrewd and crafty in his way of taking advantage of people.

When in the cursive y (7) the downstroke below the line narrows to a point,

800

this is a STING OF A WASP and the writer is given to bickering and pro-vokes, criticizes, and belittles others.

When in the cursive y (6) the part above the line begins with a long, concave, left slanting downstroke followed by a loop which is out of proportion, and when a shorter final stroke, which is not at level with the initial stroke, extends below the line and ends in a point,

801

this is an INFANT and the writer pretends helplessness to arouse the sympathy of others and to assure their aid.

When the cursive y (6) begins with a long, horizontal, initial stroke followed by a left slanting, ink-filled loop, and when a short, downward slanting stroke curves into the straight, vertical downstroke ending in a point below the line,

802

this is a BODY WITH HEAD BENT TO THE LEFT and the writer would not hesitate to slander a person, at the same time being friendly to his face.

When in the cursive y (6) a long, concave, initial downstroke re-traces the initial upstroke and forms a narrow center curve with the fol-lowing upstroke, and when the final downstroke ends in a point below the line and is slightly retraced by a straight final upstroke, which is at the right side of and close to the preceding downstroke, and ends in a point above the baseline,

803

these are CENSURING FINGERS and the writer has the tendency to ex-pose the imperfection of others and to reproach their shortcomings.

When the cursive y (6) begins with a rather long, straight or slightly convex upstroke, which is partly retraced by a shorter concave downstroke, forming a long, concave, narrow center curve with the following upstroke, and when the latter is retraced by the straight or slightly concave downstroke which is at least as long as the initial upstroke,

804

these are GRASPING FINGERS and the writer quickly takes advantage of any and every opportunity which will benefit him.

When the cursive y (6) begins with the initial downstroke, which is pointed at the top and concave, followed by a shorter upstroke curving into the final downstroke which is short above the line and may or may not have a loop below the line,

805

these are PINCH BARS and the writer would not hesitate to use force and pressure to make others pliable to his wishes.

When in the cursive y (5) the concave, initial downstroke is pointed at the top and curves into a short, downward slanting stroke, which in turn curves into the downstroke below the line, and when the latter forms a narrow loop with the final upstroke ending on the downstroke,

806

this is a DENTAL INSTRUMENT FOR FILLING CAVITIES and the writer would not hesitate to use force and pressure to coerce people into submission.

When in the cursive y (6) the downcurve or the upcurve of the part above the line is longer, and when the final downstroke ends in a point below the line,

807

these are DEVIL'S FORKS and the writer under the mask of kindness and service can cause all kinds of difficulties and confusion.

When in the cursive y (5) the loop is bulgy,

808

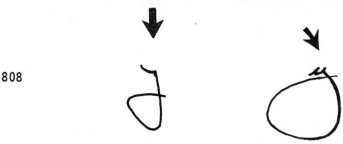

these are INFLATED LOOPS and the writer resorts to bluff to better be able to control others.

When in the cursive y (5) the final downstroke above the line is shorter or longer than the preceding, and when the lower loop is not completed and its upstroke is close to the downstroke,

809

these are WHIPS HELD DOWN and the writer has the tendency to subjugate and tyrannize people.

When in the cursive y (6) the initial downcurve is followed by the upcurve ending in an e-loop on top of the final downstroke extending into the part below the line,

810

these letters resemble the GERMAN SCRIPT H's (10) and the writer is skilled at duping and tricking people.

When the final downstroke of the cursive y (6) is straight and ends in a point below the line followed by a generously concave upstroke of the lower loop which is shaped like one-half of an ellipse and ends on the downstroke or crosses it and has a very short final stroke,

811

this is a MOON ON THE WANE IN LOWER LOOPS and the writer is changeable in his moods and his attitude towards and sympathies for people.

When in the cursive y (6, 5) a straight, final downstroke ends in a point below the line followed by a straight, left tending, upward slanting stroke, and when a right tending, final upstroke, which ends on the downstroke or may slightly cross it, forms an angle with the preceding upstroke,

812

these are TRIANGLES BELOW THE LINE and the writer uses underhanded and cruel means to weaken and control others.

When in the cursive y (6) the final downstroke, which slants far to the right, ends in a long, concave, horizontal curve below the line, and when an almost horizontal, right tending, final stroke forms an angle with the end of the preceding curve, and crosses the downstroke before it reaches the baseline,

813

this is a SINKING ROW BOAT and the writer when his patience dwindles and his zeal cools, will turn his back on all responsibility.

When in the cursive y (6), after the part above the line is made, the final downstroke ends in a point below the line followed by an almost straight upstroke of the loop, which widens at the end, curves abruptly to the right and in horizontal direction, and ends on the downstroke before it reaches the baseline,

814

this is a SAIL BOAT and the writer is fickle, apt to change his course of action as well as his sympathies for people unexpectedly.

When in the cursive y (6), after the part above the line is made, the final downstroke ends in a point below the line, and when a final upstroke, which is at the right side of the downstroke, partly retraces it and joins the next cursive e (7), which may be higher or lower than the preceding letter, and when either the final downstroke or the upstroke is curved,

815

these are BELLOWS and the writer is a show off, and to reach his objective resorts to all sorts of tricks and ruses.

When in the cursive y (6) the downstroke ends in a point below the line followed by the upstroke of the loop, which widens at the end, curves abruptly to the right before it reaches the baseline, crosses the downstroke, and slants into the loop of the next cursive e (7) or joins it, and when one of the letters is higher than the other,

816

these are LARGE SHEARS and the writer can be callous and ruthless in pursuing his aims.

When in the cursive yo (5, 7) one of the letters is higher than the other,

817

or when in the cursive ye (5, 7) the connecting line, which joins the "e" is very long,

818

these are UNUSABLE SURGICAL INSTRUMENTS and the writer is shrewd and crafty and uses all sorts of tricks and schemes to gain his ends.

Chapter 39

LETTERS OF THE ALPHABET RESEMBLING PICTORIAL FORMS: LETTERS "Z" AND "z"

When the European Z (2) has a long, straight initial upstroke which is retraced to some extent, and followed by a long, concavely curved center part and a second downstroke,

819

these are GRASPING FINGERS and the writer very quickly takes advantage of any and every opportunity which will benefit him.

When the printed Z (3) has a short upper bar and the lower bar has a generously convex curve,

820

this is a PROFILE OF NOSE WITH WIDE NOSTRILS and the writer has malicious joy in surreptitiously inflicting injury.

When the upper bar of the printed Z (3) curves into the downstroke which in turn curves into the lower bar,

821

these are STREETS WITH MANY CURVES and the writer dodges the issue in order not to be burdened with responsibility.

When the Foreign Z (4) begins with an undercurved initial upstroke in the upper half of the letter followed by the loop and the downstroke ending in a loop, and when the latter has a concave, horizontal or upward slanting final stroke,

822

229

this letter resembles the GERMAN SCRIPT h (9) and the writer can exert influence on and take advantage of people.

When in the cursive z (6) the parts above and below the line, which have narrow loops, are greater in width than in height, and when the initial and the final strokes are almost parallel,

823

this is a BODY BACKING AWAY and the writer ingratiates himself with others by lip service but wriggles out of situations which impose too much responsibility on him.

When the cursive z (7) begins with a convex, horizontal or downward slanting, initial stroke high above the baseline followed by a left tending, horizontal or downward slanting stroke curving into the part below the line which may or may not have a loop,

824

these are DENTAL INSTRUMENTS FOR DIAGNOSIS and the writer is extremely clever at sounding out people, observing the imperfection of them, and using the information to his advantage.

When the initial upstroke of the cursive z (6), which begins high above the baseline, is straight, almost horizontal and curves into a short, final downstroke above the line, and when the crossing of the loop is low,

825

this is a DEVIL'S POKER and the writer has the tendency to tyrannize and subjugate people.

When the initial upstroke of the cursive z (6) begins with a short convex or a straight horizontal stroke high above the baseline and curves into a left tending, almost horizontal stroke, and when the latter is retraced by a decidedly convex, final downstroke below the line ending in a concave horizontal curve,

826

this is the NUMBER 3 and the writer craves money and possessions so intensely that he would do anything in his power to acquire them.

Chapter 40

ARABIC NUMBERS, SIGNS, SIGNATURES, PARTITION
LINE RESEMBLING PICTORIAL FORMS

When in the printed number 1 (a) the downstroke ends in a small hook or curve turned up,

827 l

this is a RIDING CROP HELD DOWN and the writer seeks to control a situation by forcing his will on others so inconspicuously that they are not aware of his dictatorial intentions.

When the downstrokes of numbers such as "9," "1," "4," "7," narrow to a point,

828   *9147*

these are STINGS OF A WASP and the writer is given to bickering and provokes, criticizes, and belittles others.

When the number 2 (c) begins with a convex, left slanting downstroke followed by a concave, upward slanting, final stroke which has almost the same length as the preceding stroke,

829

these are SEA GULLS and the writer devises secret and underhanded plans against the interest of those who trust him.

When in the number 2 (c, b), after the initial upstroke and the downstroke are made, the latter curves into the long, final stroke which consists of a double curve or a straight line,

830   *2 2*

these are WATCHING SNAKES and the writer suspects that others might have designs on him and is looking for an opportunity to attack them unexpectedly.

When the number 2 (c), which begins with a short, initial upcurve followed by the downstroke, has a decidedly upward slanting final stroke which is at least as long as the preceding downstroke,

831

these are SWANS and the writer uses all sorts of tricks and schemes to impress people and interest them for his plans.

When the number 2 (a) begins with a short, decidedly convex downstroke followed by an indirect loop, and when the final stroke, which is decidedly convex, curves down at the point where the crossing ends and has almost the same length as the stroke preceding the loop,

832

this is a SPIDER and the writer is very smart in handling people, can win them by charm and affability, and like a spider can get them into his web.

When the two parts of the numeral 3 (a) are shaped completely different as to form and size, and when they either form an angle in the center or have a concave curve,

833

these are BODIES BACKING AWAY and the writer ingratiates himself by lip service but wriggles out of situations which impose too much responsibility on him.

When the upper indirect oval of the numeral 3 (a) begins with a long, straight, horizontal line and the lower indirect oval recedes and is wider than the upper one,

834

these are AUTHORITATIVE FINGERS and the writer has the tendency to browbeat and humiliate others.

When the initial downstroke of the number 4 (d) is convex and ends in an oblong loop followed by a straight, slightly upward slanting stroke which has almost the same length as the initial downstroke,

835

this is a SHEAF OF GRAIN and the writer has an uncanny ability to adapt himself to people, to speak their language, and to ingratiate himself so artfully with them that they believe he is on their side.

When the straight initial downstroke of the number 4 (b) joins the final downstroke at the top,

836

this is an UNFINISHED WAYSIDE SHRINE and the writer gives himself an air of faithfulness, devotedness, and friendliness but in reality is a hypocrite.

When the number 4 (d) begins with a straight, convex or concave downstroke and the horizontal line just touches the final downstroke which may be straight or curved,

837

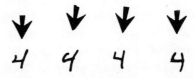

these are CHAIRS WITH BROKEN LEGS and the writer can trick, trap, and outwit people.

When in the number 4 (c) the short, initial downstroke is retraced halfway and is followed by a short, horizontal stroke which joins the final downstroke almost in the center,

838

this is a TABLE ON THE FLOOR and the writer is very selfish and mainly concerned about protecting his own interests.

When the number 4 (b) begins with the downstroke followed by the horizontal stroke, and when the final downstroke is at least as long or longer than the initial downstroke,

839

or when the first downstroke of the number 4 (b) is slightly concave and curves into the center stroke which slightly crosses the final downstroke in the upper half, and when the latter is as long as and parallel to slant of the initial downstroke,

840

these are DEVIL'S FORKS and the writer under the mask of kindness and service can cause all kinds of difficulties and confusion.

When in the number 5 (b) the upper part consists of a left tending, convex, horizontal stroke which curves into the lower part,

841

this is a WATCHING SNAKE and the writer suspects that others might have designs on him and is looking for an opportunity to attack them unexpectedly.

When in the number 5 (a, b, c) the bar is much longer than the rule stipulates and in horizontal or upward slanting position,

842

these are PELICANS and the writer tends to point out the weaknesses of others and by carping criticism undermines their self-confidence.

When in the number 5 (c) the bar stands alone or is eliminated,

843

these are SICKLES and the writer is very discontented and has the urge to inflict injury.

When the number 5 (a, b, c) begins at the baseline with a short, concave, horizontal stroke followed by an upstroke which has a double curve ending in an extremely long bar,

844

this is an INSTRUMENT OF TORTURE and the writer can harass people until they submit to his wishes.

When the loop of the number 6 (c) is not completed, not parallel to slant of the initial downstroke and ends in a horizontal curve,

845

or when in the number 6 (c), after the downstroke is made, the loop, which may or may not be completed, and may or may not touch or cross the curve resting on the baseline, is not parallel to slant of the initial downstroke,

846

these are ROLLED WHIPS and the writer wants to exert influence on and to gain control over people.

When the number 7 (a) starts with an almost circular indirect loop followed by a short bar and the final downstroke,

847

this is a RAILWAY TRAFFIC SIGNAL and the writer gives himself an air of importance by directing and guiding others and by assuming the guise of a reliable and responsible person.

When in the number 7 (b) the horizontal stroke, which may be concave, curves into or forms an angle with a decidedly concave downstroke ending in a curve turned up to the right,

848

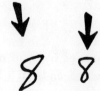

these are DEMONIAC PROFILES OF NOSES and the writer enjoys creating confusion and dissension, using schemes and plots so cunningly that no one holds him responsible.

When in the number 8 (c) the space in the upper part is wider than in the lower part, and when the final upstroke ends at the starting point,

849

these are CHESS PAWNS and the writer has the tendency to vex, humiliate and subdue others.

When the final downstroke of the number 9 (a) ends in a hook turned up to the right,

850

this is an ALGA and the writer gives the impression of agreement and co-operation but seeks to accomplish his purpose by underhanded practice.

When the oval of the number 9 (a) begins with a period within the oval followed by a short, convex upcurve, the downcurve, and a short final upcurve joining the initial upcurve,

851

this is a SPARKLING EYE and the writer tries to get himself into the good graces of others by being so fascinating and alluring that he can control them.

When the oval of the number 9 (a) begins with a generous, convex, initial upcurve to the left, and when the upcurve of the oval does not join the initial stroke and is slightly retraced by the final downstroke which is made within the oval,

852

this is an AUTO GEAR SHIFT and the writer is an autocratic person who insists on having his own will, seeks to curb and limit others, and does not easily allow them to speak their mind.

When in the number 9 (a) the upcurve of the oval is higher than the initial downcurve and is retraced by a concave downstroke, and when the oval joins the downstroke approximately in the middle,

853

this is a POT COVER and the writer wants to have his way, under all circumstances enforce his will and becomes stubborn and unreasonable when his demands are resisted or denied.

When in the $-sign (d) the upper and the lower part are differently shaped as to form and size,

854
$

this is a MEDICAL SYMBOL and the writer under the mask of readiness and willingness to help, camouflages malicious intentions.

When the bar of the printed t (6), which crosses the downstroke in the middle, has the same length as the downstroke and has two equal sides,

855
+

this is a PERFECT PLUS SIGN and the writer is good at figures.

When a signature consists of illegible letters and a horizontal or downward slanting line curves into or forms an angle with a long, left tending stroke,

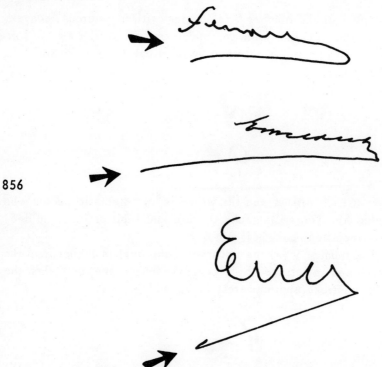

856

these are WHIPS IN SIGNATURES and the writer is so tyrannical that he would not hesitate to subjugate people and bring them into bondage.

When the partition line between numbers is long, stands alone and begins with an upward slanting double curve,

857

this is a SCYTHE and the writer is ruthless and unscrupulous.

Chapter 41

ARITHMETICAL FRACTION,
ARABIC AND ROMAN NUMERALS

When the number above an extremely long line is much smaller than the number below the line,

858

this is an UNUSUAL ARITHMETICAL FRACTION and the writer is concerned about money for himself but would not risk speculating.

When a large number is followed by two smaller "zeros" resting on the baseline,

859

the writer is generous in money and will spend it lavishly.

When one or more large numbers are followed by a sequence of "zeros" or by at least one "zero" which gets smaller in perspective towards the end,

860

the writer is very self-concerned and does nothing without hoping to benefit.

When in the number "101" the "zero" is small and may or may not rest on the baseline,

861

the writer enjoys gossiping and spreading rumors.

When in ROMAN NUMERALS (h) the upper bar is above the numerals,

862

the writer lacks patience and endurance.

When in ROMAN NUMERALS (h) the upper and lower bars slant upwards and are almost parallel,

863

the writer's self-confidence is at a low ebb.

When in ROMAN NUMERALS (h) the upper and lower bars have double curves, and when the second numeral is higher than the first one,

864

the writer uses any and every means to free himself from irksome responsibility.

When in ROMAN NUMERALS (h) the lower bar does not join the numeral,

865

the writer is a superficial observer who overlooks important details leading him to incorrect conclusions.

When in ROMAN NUMERALS (h) the two bars do not join the numerals,

866

the writer often acts so thoughtlessly that he blunders.

When in ROMAN NUMERALS (h) the lower bar slants up,

867

the writer carefully weighs the pros and cons of everything to safeguard his interests.

When in ROMAN NUMERALS (h) the upper bar slants down and the lower bar slants up,

868

the writer is distrustful and can be distant and aloof.

When in ROMAN NUMERALS (h) the bars are eliminated,

869

the writer acts without preliminary planning or thought.

When in ROMAN NUMERALS (h) the bars are at least three times as long as the stems,

870

the writer has not much initiative.

When in ROMAN NUMERALS (h) the lower bar crosses the stem,

871

the writer can be stubborn and will not listen to reason.

When in ROMAN NUMERALS (h) the stems are gradually higher,

872

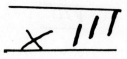

the writer can force the issue.

Chapter 42

PRELIMINARIES FOR ANALYSIS

To analyze a person's handwriting proceed with the following steps:

1) Ascertain sex and approximate age of the writer. The former is necessary to know because it cannot be determined from handwriting. The latter is necessary because many of us are not endowed with that vigor and vitality in youth as others who are advanced in years.

2) Use specimen handwritings in ink or pencil, originals or photostatic copies.

3) Use as much material as possible, for the greater the material the greater the probability of finding a large variety of features which will give a more comprehensive character portrait.

When a person writes in your presence:

4) Ask him to write on unruled paper.

5) Ask him to write one or two pages to insure relaxed penmanship.

6) Do not let him copy parts of books, magazines or newspapers.

7) Have him write innocuous questions which he is requested to answer.

8) Let him write nouns, verbs, adjectives, beginning with all the letters of the alphabet using capitals, long letters, tall letters and small letters in script and printed letters.

9) Let him write Arabic and Roman numerals.

10) Give a number to every line of the specimen handwriting to be analyzed in order to retrace your findings.

11) Do not read the context and try to concentrate on letter forms only.

12) Read only those words that are written so illegibly that you do not know to what letters of the alphabet they correspond.

13) Write down the line, the word and the letter in which you noticed a certain characteristic feature.

14) Compare and check your observation of a letter form with the illustrated example and make sure that it fits the description.

15) Jot down the interpretations for all your findings and put them into logical order.

243

Chapter 43

SAMPLE ANALYSIS

THE WRITER'S INTELLECTUAL STANDARD AND IMAGINATIVE POWER:
CHAPTER 6, SAMPLES II AND III

Line	Word	Letter	Chapter Heading Pictorial Form	Example Number
6	the	t	simple deviations from copybook models and their recognition	15
4	company	m	simple deviations from copybook models and their recognition	20a
4	stating	n	simple deviations from copybook models and their recognition	20a
8	interesting	n	simple deviations from copybook models and their recognition	20a
2	lotte	tt	simple deviations from copybook models and their recognition	3
2	letter	tt	simple deviations from copybook models and their recognition	3
2	Pap	a	simple deviations from copybook models and their recognition	17
5	a	a	simple deviations from copybook models and their recognition	17
3	Dear	D	simple deviations from copybook models and their recognition	7
2	co	c	simple deviations from copybook models and their recognition	16
4	gist	g	simple deviations from copybook models and their recognition	16
4	stating	s	simple deviations from copybook models and their recognition	16
7	me	m	the slant of the writing	42
1	must	m	the slant of the writing	42
7	end	n	the slant of the writing	42
3	Dear	r	the slant of the writing	44
7	from	r	the slant of the writing	44
8	or	r	the slant of the writing	44
8	interesting	nn,tt	the slant of the writing	38
5	secondly	n, dl	the slant of the writing	38
5	company	p, y	the slant of the writing	38
8	lit	i	the i-dots	50
1	it	i	the i-dots	54
8	interesting	i	the i-dots	52
1	number	8	punctuation marks	61
2	lotte	e	punctuation marks	61
4	company		connections and separations	77
6	privilege		connections and separations	77
8	interesting		connections and separations	77
1	Pap	P	connections and separations	80
4	company		alignment of letters and words	87
5	Secondly		alignment of letters and words	91
7	be	e	alignment of letters and words	90
1	must	m	alignment of letters and words	88
5	for	r	initial and final strokes	101

(Continued)

Line	Word	Letter	Chapter Heading Pictorial Form	Example Number
4	to	t	initial and final strokes	94, 95
7	from	f	initial and final strokes	94, 95
5	for	f	initial and final strokes	94, 95
8	interesting	i	initial and final strokes	94, 95
6	the	t	initial and final strokes	94, 95
6	the	e	initial and final strokes	110
6	first "to"	t	imperfect plus sign	719
1	number	8	chess pawn	849
1	number "1"		sting of a wasp	828
1	number "5"		pelican	842
1		N	profile of broad nose	509
2	Boy	B	warning finger	162
2	lotte	tte	pierced fingers	749
2	letter	tte	pierced fingers	749
8	lit	it	unusable anchor	368
7	be	b	pointed finger	164
2	Pap	P	whip held up	583
8	the	t	riding crop held to the right	712
8	interesting	t	riding crop held to the right	712
2	lotte	te	spider	732
2	lotte	te	number 6	734
3	the	he	spider	350
3	har	a	number 6	146
2	lotte	o	number 6	517
3	Dear	D	loops extending beyond the letter	178
5	for	f	left tending additional loop on the line	244
2	co	o	broken egg shell	521
3	of	f	knife	268
4	of	f	knife	545
3	of	o	Quiver	545
4	to	o	Quiver	545
6	off	o	Quiver	545
7	from	f	Quiver	255
8	the	h	sharp beak	337
3	so	o	sly eye	540
5	Secondly	o	sly eye	540
4	gest	t	bow and arrow	723
4	stating	tat	high stage	687
4	to	t	gallow to the right	709
6	to	t	gallow to the right	709
5	a	a	parasite	127
5	to	o	pebble	549
5	Secondly	y	pinch bar	805
6	privilege	ge	unusable surgical instrument	306
5	company	o, a	complete and incomplete circles and/or eclipses	520
6	to	t, o	lamp with goose-neck	742

(concluded)

Line	Word	Letter	Chapter Heading Pictorial Form	Example Number
6	second "to"	o	small fish	522
7	end	d	unusable propeller blade	201
7	I've	e	infant	230
8	or	o	spade	547
4	stating	g	peculiarities in pen pressure	73
4	company	y	peculiarities in pen pressure	73

873

1 *must no 8, 15 it*

2 *Co Boy Pag letter, letter*

3 *its has Dear of so*

4 *of gist stating to company*

5 *for a company to Secondly*

6 *privilege to the to off*

7 *end I've be me from*

8 *interesting the or lit*

The following sample analysis was purposely worked out from a specimen handwriting cut into words to familiarize the student to ignore the content and concentrate wholly on the essential components.

In this exhaustive analysis I want to demonstrate that character traits and tendencies which we are accustomed to think of as undesirable and objectionable can turn into assets under certain circumstances and are necessary for self-protecting reasons. As long as a person contributes to achievement in public life and in the community, we should be understanding and sensible enough to be contented with him and not have expectations that a person cannot fulfill because he cannot change his nature.

The writer of the specimen handwriting No. 873, page 246, is endowed with natural intelligence. He is prosaic and matter of fact.

Without much effort on his part, he can adapt himself to a variety of people and situations never losing perspective and sight of his underlying purpose. Mixing with and contacting many people is his forte. He is smart in handling people and able to win them by charm and affability. He finds it easy to sound out people and gain information which will be of value to him. He is a trickster and resorts to skillful maneuvers as the easiest way out of difficulties. He uses white lies to back out of unwelcome situations and can say the opposite of what he really means so subtly and unnoticeably that no one suspects him of deceit.

Since he can keep others in the dark about his true intentions, it will be difficult for most people to figure him out. One of his machinations is pretended helpfulness to arouse the sympathy of others and to assure their aid. The guileless and naive impression he conveys aids him in his dealings with people.

No doubt, he has salesmanship and through tricks and ruses can impress those customers who fall for showmen and people who can put on an act successfully. Although he can be considered two-faced, by conveying the impression of being sincere, congenial and unselfish, he can achieve professional success. However, he can also employ other means to achieve mastery of people and situations. He can control them by forcible means to attain his objective.

In spite of the fact that at times his pride is hurt by those customers who have slighted him, he tries to contact them again and re-establish friendly relations. Being an opportunist, he wins out in situations where many lose because they cannot compromise. He excels in cunning and therefore controls situations where sincere and honest people are bound to fail. He makes promises but with mental reservations. He may agree to a proposition but might not live up to his obligations. He is at his best if he can slyly take advantage of people. He is inordinately selfish and greedy, craves money and possessions so intensely that he would do anything in his power to acquire them. He wants an easy life at the expense of others and has little power of resistance against temptations.

Since he is not burdened with warm feelings for others, he can be so cold, icy and callous that he can easily rid himself of persons who are in his way or whom he dislikes for other reasons. This character trait can be considered an asset in his battle for eliminating competition.

He is much less suited for administrative or research work because he is not thorough, not patient, not accurate enough in his work.

Then, too, there is a great discrepancy between his thinking and acting. He grasps things quickly but often lacks the power of decision, the vigor, and the initiative to put his knowledge into action. Then his zeal cools and his working power diminishes. He becomes distracted, forgetful and indifferent.

If a person is wanted who can exercise authority and coerce people into submission, he is the right man. However, in his relations with partners, co-workers or subordinates frictions may arise for the following reasons: He does not assume the responsibility for faults and is prone to put the blame on others. He enjoys exposing people, making them objects of ridicule, pointing out their weaknesses and by carping criticism undermines their self-confidence. Although he gives the impression of being lamb-like, he is always tensed to pounce and can unexpectedly become harsh and antagonistic. Then, too, he finds it difficult to forget a wrong and would retaliate by inflicting injury surreptitiously. He can be friendly to a person's face and hide malicious and perfidious designs by pretended friendship.

He cannot inspire co-workers nor can he strengthen their self-confidence. He can easily lose their respect because he does not adhere to an opinion once formed. He is not tough-minded and has times when he does not know what he wants so that others do not acknowledge his suggestions and his prestige is apt to decline.

To handle this sensitive person with great courtesy and affability will pay dividends. To reproach him for failures may evoke his revenge. Once he loses interest in and enthusiasm for his work, he will throw up the game and will quit his job.

In his professional life this man can easily adapt himself to society. However, in his private life he is not an easy person. Although he conveys the impression of safeguarding the interest of others, he is a downright egotist and will not make an easy consort. He is given to bickering and provokes, criticizes and belittles others. His patience with others is limited. At times when he is upset, he will not only misconstrue the honest intentions of others but also resent them. As a matter of fact, he lacks a sense of humor, loathes being the butt of a joke, and will easily lose his composure.

He is uncurably romantic and not the faithful or loyal type. The interest women show in him boosts his male ego. Since he is very conceited, he can be an easy prey for women who know how to flatter him. Since he is a hypocrite and inclined to misrepresent facts, he would need a wife not cursed with jealousy, one who does not demand veracity.

Due to his feelings of inadequacy, he tries to impress his world as a strong man. However, he can be controlled by a woman who holds him on a long leash and can make him believe that he is the master of the house. A woman who would try to boss him and curtail his freedom of action would be the loser. Then, the negative side of his nature would come to the fore and he would resort to force to make his wishes prevail. He would need a tactful and diplomatic woman who, when he is childish and unreasonable, does not reprimand him but rather looks up to him and shows her appreciation of him. By paying homage to him, she can make him more enterprising and help him overcome periods of passivity and boredom. However, she would have to assume a secondary role and repress many a wish by letting him feel that she is his subject.

This man has an unceasing longing for freedom but since he has not yet reached full maturity, he needs guidance. Only then will he succeed and become a more integrated human being.

BIBLIOGRAPHY

Allport, G. W. and P. E. Vernon: *Studies in Expressive Movement.* New York, Macmillan Co., 1933.

Anderson, H. H. and G. L. Anderson (Eds.): *An Introduction to Projective Techniques.* Englewood Cliffs, N. J., Prentice-Hall, Inc., 1951.

Anthony, D. S.: *Digest of Workshop.* San Jose, Calif., American Handwriting Analysis Foundation, 1960.

Bell, J. E.: *Projective Techniques.* New York, Longmanns, Green & Co., 1948.

Booth, G. C.: The use of graphology in medicine. *J. Nerv. Ment. Dis.,* 1937.

Booth, G. C.: Objective techniques in personality testing. *Arch. Neurol. Psychiat,* 1939.

Cantril, H., H. A. Rand, and G. W. Allport: *The Determination of Personal Interests by Psychological and Graphological Methods,* 1933.

Castelnuovo-Tedesco, P.: A study of the relationship between handwriting and personality variables, *Genet. Psychol. Monogr.,* 1948.

Crepieux-Jamin, J.: *Les éléments de l'écriture des canailles.* Paris, Presses Universitaires, 1924.

Crepieux-Jamin, J.: *L'écriture et le caractère.* Paris, Presses Universitaires, 1947.

Crepieux-Jamin, J.: *The Psychology of the Movements of Handwriting.* London, G. Routledge H Sons, Ltd., 1926.

Downey, June E.: *Graphology and the Psychology of Handwriting.* Baltimore, Warwick & York, 1919.

Farberow, Norman L.: *Taboo Topics.* New York, Atherton Press, 1963.

Flückiger, F. A., C. A. Tripp, and G. H. Weinberg: A review of experimental research in graphology, 1933-1960, *Percept. Motor Skills, Monogr. Suppl.,* 1961.

Goodenough, Florence L.: Sex differences in judging the sex of handwriting, *J. Soc. Psychol.,* 1945.

Hager, William: *Genetische Graphologie; die Persönlichkeit im Wandel der Handschrift.* München, J. A. Barth, 1957.

Hull, C. L. and Ruth P. Montgomery: Experimental investigation of certain alleged relations between character and handwriting, *Psychol. Rev.,* 1919.

Jacobi, Hans J.: *Self-knowledge Through Handwriting.* London, J. M. Dent & Sons, Ltd., 1941.

Kanfer, A. and D. F. Casten: Observations on disturbances in neuro-muscular coordination in patients with malignant disease, *Bull. Hosp. Joint Dis.* (N.Y.), 1958.

Klages, L.: *Ausdrucksbewegung and Gestaltungskraft.* Leipzig, J. A. Barth, 1923.

Klages, L.: *Handschrift und Charakter.* Leipzig, J. A. Barth, 1936.

Knobloch, Hans: *Die Lebensgestalt der Schrift.* Saarbrücken, West-Ost Verlag, 1950.

Langenbruch, W.: *Praktische Menschenkenntnis auf Grund der Handschrift.* Berlin, Kameradschaft G. m. b. h., 1911.

Lewinson, Thea Stein and J. Zubin: *Handwriting Analysis.* New York, King's Crown Press, 1942; reprinted by University Microfilm, Inc., Ann Arbor, Mich., 1963.

Mendel, Alfred O.: *Personality in Handwriting.* New York, Stephen Daye Press, 1947.

Michon, J. H.: *Les mystères de l'écriture.* Paris, Presses Universitaires, 1872.

Michon, J. H.: *Système de Graphology, l'art de connaître les hommes d'après leur écriture.* Paris, Presses Universitaires, 1875.

Müller, William H. and Alice Enskat: *Graphologische Diagnostik.* Bern and Stuttgart, Hans Huber, 1961.

Pascal, G. R.: The analysis of handwriting: a test of significance. *Character & Personality,* 1943.

Pascal, G. R.: Handwriting pressure: its measurement and significance. *Character and Personality,* 1943.

Pfanne, Heinrich: *Lehrbuch der graphologischen Psychodiagnostik auf Grund graphologischer Komplexe.* Berlin, Walter-De-Gruyter, 1960.

Pokorny, Richard R.: *Die Moderne Handschriftendeutung.* Berlin, Walter-De-Gruyter.

Pophal, Rud: *Zur Psychologie der Spannungserscheinungen in der Handschrift.* Der Greifenverlag, 1949.

Pophal, Rud: *Das Strichbild zum Form und Stoffproblem in der Psychologie der Handschrift.* Stuttgart, G. Thieme, 1960.

Preyer, W.: *Zur Psychologie des Schreibens.* Hamburg and Leipzig, L. Voss, 1919.

Pulver, Max Albert Eugen: *Symbolik der Handschrift.* Zürich, O. Füssli, 1931.

Roman, Klara G.: Handwriting and speech: a study of the diagnostic value of graphic indices for the exploration of speech disorders, *Logos,* 1959.

Roman, Klara G.: *Handwriting-A Key to Personality.* New York, Pantheon Books, Inc., 1952.

Roman, Klara G.: Graphology, in *Encyclopedia Mental Health.* New York, Grolier, 1963.

Saudek, Robert: *The Psychology of Handwriting.* London, G. Allen & Unwin, Ltd., 1925.

Secord, P. F.: Studies of the relationship of handwriting to personality. *J. Personality,* 1949.

Sonnemann, Ulrich: *Handwriting Analysis as a Psychodiagnostic Tool.* London, G. Allen & Unwin, Ltd., 1952.

Tripp, C. A., F. A. Flückiger and G. H. Weinberg: Effects of alcohol on the graphomotor performances of normals and chronic alcoholics. *Percept. Motor Skills,* 1959.

Wieser, Roda: *Persönlichkeit und Handschrift.* München, E. Reinhardt, 1956.

Wieser, Roda: *Mensch und Leistung in der Handschrift* München, E. Reinhardt, 1960.

Wintermantel, F.: *Bibliographia graphologica.* Stuttgart, Ruhle-Diebener Verlag K. G., 1957.

Wolff, W.: *Diagrams of the Unconscious.* New York, Grune & Stratton, 1948.

Wolfson, Rose: *A Study in Handwriting Analysis.* Ann Arbor, Mich., Edwards Bros., Inc., 1949.

Wolfson, Rose: Graphology; in H. H. Anderson & Gladys L. Anderson, Eds.: *An Introduction to Projective Techniques.* Englewood Cliffs, N. J., Prentice-Hall, Inc., 1951.

INDEX OF DEVIATIONS FROM THE STANDARD
AND THEIR NAMES: By Numbers and Letters

A

"a" size of the letter (*see* Small Letters)
Acorn, 124-a
Additional Loops (*see* Loops)
Airplane
circling to the right, 328-H
circling to the left, 327-H
Airship, grounded, 555-of
Algae, 179-D, 278-G, 279-G, 280-g, 425-1 (letter), 466-M, 467-m, 500-N, 607-r, 627-S, 859-9
Alignment
of letter parts, 88
of two "f's," 92
of words or parts of a word, 86, 87, 88, 89, 90, 91, 93
Anchor, unusable, 175-c, 368-il, 432-1 (letter), 754-ut
Angle Iron, 654-Th
Anther, 441-ll (letters)
Antique Lock Plate (*see* Lock Plate)
Antique Sword
lifted (*see* Sword)
lowered (*see* Sword)
Anvil, 551-oc, 777-wi
Arabic Numbers (*see* Numbers)
Arabic Numerals (*see* Numerals)
Architectural Style (*see* Style)
Arithmetical Fraction (*see* Fraction)
Arm
enticing, 656-T, 657-T
encircling, 526-of
Authoritative Finger (*see* Finger)
Auto Gear Shift, 199-d, 273-G, 397-K, 577-P, 598-R, 852-9
Automatic Warning Bell (*see* Bell)
Axe (*see* Ice Ax)

B

Bamboo Gate, 655-TT
Banner, 703-tt
Bar
resembling a dash (*see* Dash)
Barbed Hook (*see* Hook)
Beak
dull, 338-h, 413-L, 741-t
of a duck, 608-r
sharp, 337-h, 412-L
Bell
automatic warning out of order, 202-d

clapper of a, 642-so
Bellow, 276-Ge, 277-ge, 423-L, 424-ll (letters), 641-sh, 662-T, 663-te, 815-ye
Belt Buckle, 221-E
Bird
head of a, 112-A, 643-T, 798-y
with wings expanded, 609-r
Blade
of a dagger, 166-b, 349-h, 410-k, 667-T, 668-t
of a hacksaw, 486-mn
of a propeller, unusable, 168-b, 201-d, 254-f, 379-J
of a fan, 264-f
Boat
row, 329-H, 357-I, 721-t
sail, 302-g, 814-y
sinking row, 301-g, 382-J, 813-y
torpedo, 559-oi, 780-wi
Body
backing away, 823-Z, 833-3
graceful, 215-E
leaning back, 129-a, 562-on, 563-or
provocative, 227-E, 613-r
rear view of a, 387-J
sensuous, 291-g
squirming, 228-ei en er
with arm rested, 614-r
with chest out head back, 214-E
with head bent forward, 251-f, 390-j, 593-p
with head bent to the left, 802-y
with outstretched legs, 216-E
Bow and Arrow, 722-t, 723-t, 783-X
Bracket, 172-C, 188-D, 361-I, 362-i, 399-K, 435-I, (letter), 669-Tt
Brad-Awl, 117-A
Broad Profile of Nose (*see* Profile of Nose)
Broken Egg Shell (*see* Egg Shell)
Broken Saber (*see* Saber)
Broken Sleigh (*see* Sleigh)
Bull's Horn (*see* Horn)
Bubbles, 208-de
Buttock, deformed, 775-w

C

"c" resembling the cursive "E," 173
Candle
with flickering flame, 204-d, 430-1 (letter)

INDEX OF CHARACTERISTICS:

By Pages